A Celebration of Stitching

A Special Collection Of Needlecraft Creations From More Than 70 Designers Worldwide

WITHDRAWN

Published by

krause publications

700 East State Street • Iola, WI 54990-0001
715/445-2214 • FAX: 715/445-4087   www.krause.com

Please call or write for our free catalog of publications. Our toll-free number to place an order or obtain a free catalog is 800-258-0929 or please use our regular business telephone 715-445-2214 for editorial comment and further information.

Library of Congress Catalog Number 00-111292
ISBN 0-87349-284-6

Welcome to
A Celebration of Stitching...

The book that you are holding in your hands is a very special one. It was created as a positive and beautiful way to celebrate the creativity of the needlework industry, while also trying to raise awareness about the potential threat of copyright violations.

More than 70 designers from all around the world took part in this adventure. Each of them generously donated a small design celebrating their unique style, favorite subject matter, or stitching techniques. Some of the names on these pages will already be very familiar to you, while others offer a wealth of talent and creativity that you may be discovering for the first time.

Designers chose their colors from a common Color Key (see page 6), making these projects much easier to follow, stitch, or mix and match. Each designer was free to add embellishments, specialty threads, metallics, beads, or other wonders to their creation to enhance the basic colors chosen.

This book also marked the first time that so many people within the needlework industry worked together to bring something like this to life. From designers, the publisher, and suppliers to industry trade magazines, organizations, distributors, and store owners—everyone gave of their time and resources to ensure that as much money as possible from this publication goes toward the Copyright Protection Fund to protect the industry that we all love. This fund will be used to educate stitchers about copyright issues and protect it from serious violations affecting the industry as a whole. You will find some of the basic copyright information and issues addressed in the pages of this book.

A Celebration of Stitching would never have been possible without the efforts of those who worked so hard to put it all together, including the members of the original INRG Legal Defense Fund Committee, as it was first called when the idea for this project was born during the summer Charlotte 2000 INRG show. Krause Publications generously donated its considerable time and talents in editing, designing, and paginating the treasury of designs which you now hold in your hands.

So come... dream of the possibilities... pick out your colors... thread your needle... and celebrate with every stitch!

INRG Legal Defense Fund Committee Members:
• Jennifer L. Aikman-Smith of Dragon Dreams
• Cheri Barton of Black Swan Designs
• Tink Boord-Dill of Tink Boord-Dill Needlework
• Peg Edwards of Carolina Country House
• Jim Hedgepath of Pegasus Web Productions
• Sharon Wainright of Sew Original
• Letha Welch of Fantasy Crafts

A Message from
Krause Publications

Krause Publications is pleased to participate in this worthy endeavor. As a publisher, we appreciate the importance of the protection we receive under copyright law—we would cease to exist without its protection. Unless we create under that protection, our books could be easily copied, used, or re-published by others. When it is our work, others do not have the right to use it without our permission.

Needlework designers are equally protected under this law. Their individual creations are theirs alone to sell or license. We are all bound by law to observe this protection and not copy, sell, or claim as ours any work that we did not design.

It is important to educate those who do not understand this law and thus take advantage of others out of ignorance. It is important to send a legal and financial message to those who understand this law and willfully ignore it; they shall be the targets of our legal action. The proceeds of this book are intended to support the actions required to change the illegal practices of those stealing and copying the works of independent designers.

It is important to secure this protection in order to allow designers to earn a fair wage through their creative designs. It is important to protect our industry so that it draws creative people to it rather than discourages them from participating. And it is important to send a moral message about right and wrong. We're pleased to be able to share our time, effort, and enthusiasm in this effort.

Together, we can restore a creative atmosphere of respect and just adherence to both the intent and letter of the copyright law. Join us today. Do not photocopy or accept designs that are protected under copyright. Do not accept or forward computer designs that someone other than the designer sends to you. And ask your friends to follow this law as well.

Pat Klug
Manager, Book Division

Table of Contents

Main Color Key

Sym	DMC	Anchor	Description
⊗	309	42	Rose - deep
8	311	148	Navy Blue - med
◪	334	977	Baby Blue - med
☑	367	217	Pistachio Green - dk
⊓	368	214	Pistachio Green - lt
Ⅱ	369	1043	Pistachio Green - vy lt
H	498	1005	Christmas Red - dk
N	500	683	Blue Green - vy dk
:	501	878	Blue Green - dk
M	502	877	Blue Green
+	504	1042	Blue Green - vy lt
◆	550	102	Violet - vy dk
3	552	99	Violet - med
◨	554	96	Violet - lt
Ⅸ	646	8581	Beaver Grey - dk
C	648	900	Beaver Grey - lt
−	676	891	Old Gold - lt
⌂	729	890	Old Gold - med
2	740	316	Tangerine
L	743	302	Yellow - med
⊠	744	301	Yellow - pale

Sym	DMC	Anchor	Description
◱	776	24	Pink - med
▲	814	45	Garnet - dk
⊡	819	271	Baby Pink - lt
▣	839	360	Beige Brown - dk
6	841	378	Beige Brown - lt
⊙	842	388	Beige Brown - vy lt
Z	844	1041	Beaver Grey - ul dk
☺	890	218	Pistachio Green - ul dk
⊟	899	52	Rose - med
▼	931	1034	Antique Blue - med
V	932	1033	Antique Blue - lt
■	939	152	Navy Blue - vy dk
♥	947	330	Burnt Orange
⊡	3031	360	Mocha Brown - vy dk
I	3072	847	Beaver Grey - vy lt
▦	3325	129	Baby Blue - lt
n	3750	1036	Antique Blue - vy dk
⌐	3753	1031	Antique Blue - ul vy lt
0	3823	386	Ultra Pale Yellow
⊟	3829	901	Old Gold - vy dk
·	5200	1	Snow White

We wanted to make it easy for you to mix and match designs in this book, so, wherever possible, designers tried to match or adapt the symbols of their various charting programs to this main symbol/color key. Designers were free to add any specialty fibers, beads, metallics, buttons, or other embellishments they wanted to their pieces. These are marked with a ❖ beside the symbol on each individual page. This way, you will know what else you need to have on hand besides the floss colors listed here.

❖ *Copyright Information*

What is a copyright?

Copyrights are meant to protect creativity once it becomes something tangible. You can't copyright an idea, inspiration, or even a fact, but the minute it has been brought to life, painted, carved, composed, written, stitched, or captured in some way, it belongs to the person who created it and is protected.

During the Berne Copyright Convention, almost every major country in the world agreed that copyright occurs the minute something gets created, whether or not it gets registered with a copyright office or has the copyright symbol beside it (although these are both ways to protect something further). In most cases, this copyright lasts until 50 years after the author/creator dies.

What rights does a creator have?

Under copyright law, the owner or creator of the work has what are called Owner's Exclusive Rights. These cover the rights to:
❖ Reproduction
❖ Creation of a Derivative Work (using elements of one image/song/poem/ story to create a new one)
❖ Distribution (publication or distribution including physically or electronically)
❖ Display (whether the physical creation or an image of that creation)

The only person who can grant permission for any of these actions to take place is the creator or copyright holder.

This sounds very black and white, but the reality of dealing with copyright issues is that there seem to be many gray areas.

What about Fair Use?

The Fair Use clause (or Fair Dealing, in Canada and several other countries) was designed to allow critics to quote passages of books or show clips of films when reviewing them. It also allows educators to copy materials when used for teaching purposes, under certain guidelines.

This clause has often been used to justify the copying and sharing of designs in the needlecraft industry. Some needlecraft designers allow a working copy to be made from their charts so that stitchers don't have to mark up the original chart while stitching. Other designers prefer that you do mark up the original if necessary and offer replacement charts. Check the chart for details (such as permission to copy the chart for personal use) or contact the designer directly. These are the best ways to find out what the copyright owner prefers.

If I bought it, can't I do whatever I want with my pattern or kit?

Yes... for the most part. When you buy a paperback book, you have the right to keep it on your bookshelf, loan it to a friend, donate it to your local library/church/

school, etc., or sell it in your yard sale. You have purchased the physical product, and it is up to you what you do with it. But this is where technology makes things tricky. If you make a copy of the original, like a photocopy or digital scan, you do not have the right to share, sell, or trade that copy in any way. The only thing you "own" is the physical copy of the original. The moment that a copy or scan is made (except where permission for personal use is granted), the copyright has been broken. Sharing or distributing that image freely is not only a further violation of the Owner's Exclusive Rights, under the distribution category, it also has the potential to seriously harm this industry that we all enjoy. That is why this book has come into being.

What's a Derivative Work? Is that when I put different elements from patterns together?

No one can copyright an idea... and sometimes ideas get interpreted in similar ways, especially with combinations of stitches rather than images. Copyrights also protect a creator from having recognizable elements of their work copied or used in other images known as "derivative works."

Stitchers are perfectly free to combine elements from various patterns to create something unique for their own pleasure or as a gift; however, no one can copy parts of an existing design or knowingly incorporate them into a new design and then claim them as their own, especially if the new design is being reproduced for profit or shared freely. This also protects the images of artists, photographers, sculptors, designers, etc. from being adapted into other forms like needlework, without their knowledge or consent. You could convert a photograph you took or painting you created into cross stitch, but you couldn't download a painting or image off the web and create a pattern from it without the artist's permission, especially if you were going to sell or share the pattern.

Can't I display photos of things I have stitched on a personal website?

Under the strict letter of copyright law, unless you have the designer's permission, the answer would be no. There are probably as many opinions on this as there are designers, so it helps to check with them before you do it. Most will probably request that the design is properly attributed to them (i.e. putting the title of the design and the designer's name near the image) or that you make sure the image is not "reproduction quality" so that someone who was intent on breaking the copyright of an image couldn't get his or her hands on it.

What's the bottom line?

If you aren't the one who created the image, wrote the story, composed the song, or programmed the code, then you need permission before you reproduce material in any form. Sometimes this permission is included in a licensing agreement or copyright disclaimer, but if the information is not available, you must check with the copyright holder before breaking any of the Owner's Exclusive Rights.

Anne Brinkley

"ROSES AND BLUEBELLS"

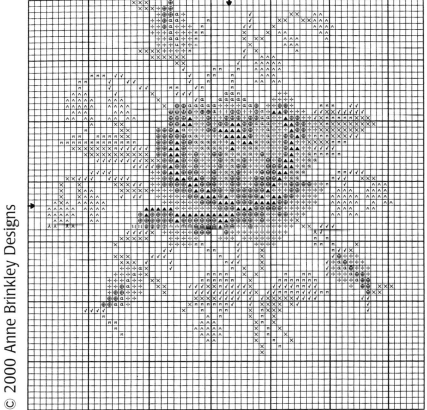

Stitch Count: 58w x 59h

This project was stitched over one on 28-count antique white Zweigart Cashel Linen using one strand of floss. The final stitching dimensions are 2 inches wide x 2 inches high.

Project Color Key

	DMC	ANCHOR	
⊗	309	42	Rose-DK
☑	367	217	Pistachio Grn-DK
⊡	368	214	Pistachio Grn-LT
ⓐ	776	24	Pink-MD
▲	814	45	Garnet-DK
⊕	890	218	Pistachio Grn-UL DK
⊟	899	52	Rose-MD
⌒	3753	1031	Ant. Blue-UL VY LT

Anne Brinkley Designs
3895 B N. Oracle Rd.
Tucson, AZ 85705
1-800-633-0148 or 520-888-1642
fax 520-888-1483
e-mail: annebrinkleydes@aol.com

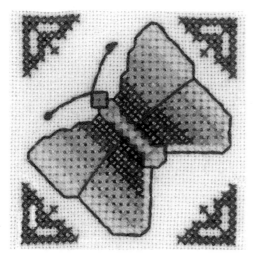

❖ *Another Time Designs*

Virginia Ramirez

"CELEBRATION BUTTERFLY"

Stitch Count: 30 x 30

This project was stitched over two on 28-count antique white Zweigart Jubilee using two strands of floss.

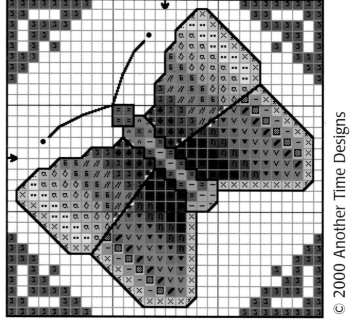

Project Color Key

Floss Used for Full Stitches:

	DMC	ANCHOR	
⊠	311	148	Navy Blue - med
◢	334	977	Baby Blue - med
◆	550	102	Violet - vy dk
③	552	99	Violet - med
⊘	554	96	Violet - lt
⊟	676	891	Old Gold - lt
⬠	729	890	Old Gold - med
⊠	744	301	Yellow - pale
⊡	776	24	Pink - med

	DMC	ANCHOR	
⊡	819	271	Baby Pink - lt
⑤	841	378	Beige Brown - lt
⊗	842	388	Beige Brown - vy lt
▼	931	1034	Antique Blue - med
⩔	932	1033	Antique Blue - lt
■	939	152	Navy Blue - vy dk
▩	3325	129	Baby Blue - lt
⋔	3750	1036	Antique Blue - vy dk
⌁	3753	1031	Antique Blue - ul vy lt
⊟	3829	901	Old Gold - vy dk

Floss Used for Backstitches:

	DMC	ANCHOR	
◿	844	1041	Beaver Grey - ul dk

Floss Used for French Knots:

	DMC	ANCHOR	
●	844	1041	Beaver Grey - ul dk

Another Time Designs
1524 Pinto Court
Carson City, NV 89701
website: www.anothertimedesigns.com

❖ *Black Swan Designs*

Cheri Barton & Karen Weaver

"FLIGHT OF FANCY"

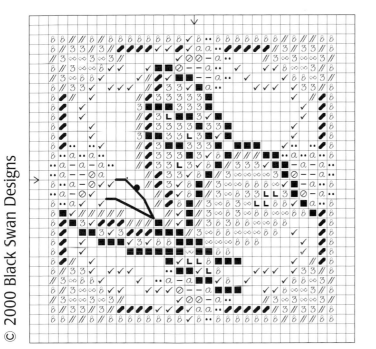

Stitch Count: 30 x 30

This project was stitched over two on 28-count antique white Zweigart Jubilee. Two strands were used when stitching with the DMC floss. Use two strands of 939 when backstitching the antennae.

Project Color Key

	DMC	ANCHOR	
⊠	309	42	Rose Dark
⊟	311	148	Navy Blue Medium
⊿	334	977	Baby Blue Medium
☑	367	216	Pistachio Green Dark
◈	550	101	Violet Very Dark
③	552	99	Violet Medium
⊘	554	95	Violet Light
⌊	743	302	Yellow Medium
⊡	776	24	Pink Medium
⠂⠂	819	271	Baby Pink Light
⊟	899	38	Rose Medium
■	939	152	Navy Blue Very Dark

P.O. Box 67
Fort Mill, SC 29715
e-mail: cwbofbsd@aol.com
website: www.blackswandesigns.com

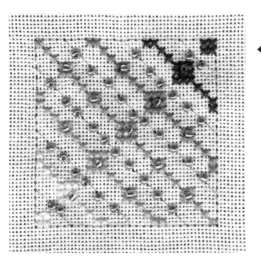

❖ *Bunny Tales Cross Stitch Design*

Bunny Goodman

"SIMPLY ELEGANT"

Stitch Count: 25 x 25

This project was stitched over two on 28-count antique white Zweigart Cashel Linen. Two strands were used when stitching with the DMC floss, while only one strand was used when stitching with the Kreinik Japan Thread.

Pink beads are attached with one strand of DMC 819, stitching through the bead hole twice. Gold beads are attached with one strand of Japan Thread, stitching through the bead hole twice.

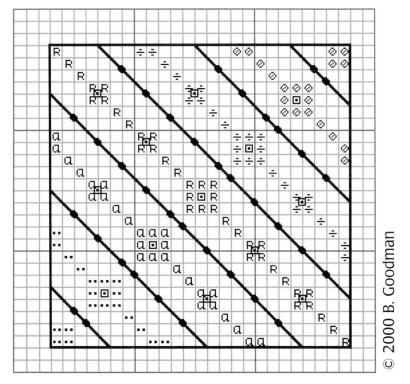

Bunny Tales Cross Stitch Design

P.O. Box 2103, Station A
Nanaimo, British Columbia, Canada
V9R 6X9
250-753-9765

Project Color Key

	DMC	ANCHOR	
⊗	309	42	Rose Deep
ⓐ	776	24	Pink Medium
⊡	819	271	Baby Pink Light
⊟	899	52	Rose Medium
Ⓡ	One strand of 776/24 + one strand of 899/52		
❖ ◉	00557 Mill Hill Glass Gold Seed Bead		
❖ ▣	03050 Mill Hill Antique Pink Glass Bead		
❖ ◪	Backstitch with one strand Kreinik 002J Gold Japan Thread		

❖ *Carolina Country House*

Peg Edwards

"CELTIC KNOT"

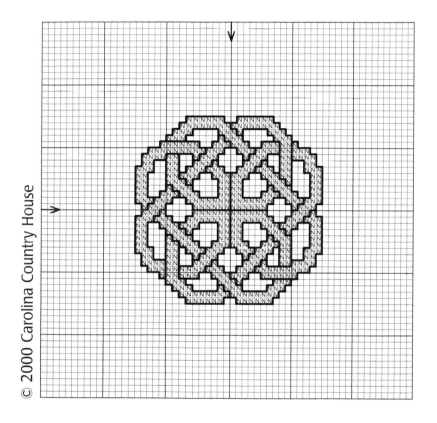

Stitch Count: 30 x 30

This project was stitched over two on 28-count antique white Zweigart Cashel Linen. Two strands of the DMC floss were used for the cross stitches, and one strand of the Kreinik #12 Gold Braid was used in the backstitching.

This lovely design can easily be adapted to suit any color scheme by choosing a different color of floss or braid.

Project Color Key

	DMC	ANCHOR	
N	500	683	Very Dark Blue Green
❖ ⧄	Backstitch single strand with Kreinik #12 Gold Braid, color number 002		

Carolina Country House
10326 Hollybrook Dr.
Charlotte, NC 28277
e-mai: needlework@aol.com
website:
www.carolinacountryhouse.com

❖ *Cat's Cradle Needleworks*

Juliet Anne Jones

"A CELEBRATION OF STITCHING"

Stitch Count: 34w x 24h

This project was stitched on 28-count antique white Cashel Linen. Cross stitch over two threads using two strands of floss. Backstitch the ring around the milk bowl using one strand of Kreinik 002P Balger Cable. Backstitch the cats' collars in two strands of Kreinik 002P Balger Cable. Backstitch the cats' outline in DMC 939 using one strand of floss. Backstitch "love" in Weeks Dye Works 2337 Periwinkle, using two strands. Stitch the cats' eyes in Kreinik 002P Balger Cable. This piece can be stitched into a heart-shaped pillow and hung from a doorknob using Periwinkle twisted cord.

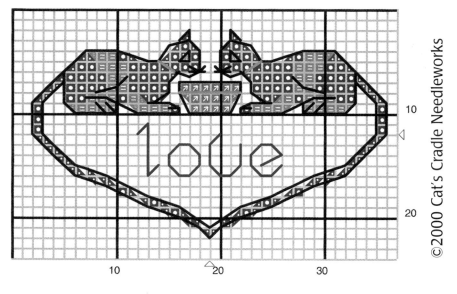

©2000 Cat's Cradle Needleworks

HC 88 Box 114D
513 Forest Dr.
Pocono Lake, PA 18347-9731

Project Color Key

	DMC	ANCHOR	
■	939	152	Navy Blue - vy dk
⊟	3829	901	Old Gold - vy dk
•	Weeks Dye Works 2337 Periwinkle		
↗	Thread Gatherer SNC 047 Willow Green		
◆	Kreinik 002P Balger Cable		

❖*A Celebration of Stitching*

© 2000 JLAS

Stitch Count: 30 x 30

This project was stitched over two on 28-count antique white Zweigart Cashel Linen.

This block is an ideal centerpiece for those combining their favorite squares into a larger design or a round-robin project. It can be stitched as a floral motif with the colors as shown below, or as an abstract design incorporating your favorite colors. Feel free to be creative if the spirit moves you...

Project Color Key

	DMC	ANCHOR	
⦂	501	878	Blue Green Dark
M	502	877	Blue Green
+	504	1042	Blue Green Very Light
◲	776	24	Pink Medium
⚬⚬	819	271	Baby Pink Light
÷	899	52	Rose Medium
⬕	Backstitch with a single strand of floss in the color of your choice. DMC 30930 Rayon floss was used in the model shown above.		

How to Donate to the Copyright Protection Fund

If you would like to make a further donation to help protect this industry from copyright abuse, please contact:

Jim Hedgepath
e-mail: jim@pegweb.com

Sandra Richardson

"CELESTIAL MINIATURE"

Stitch Count: 30 x 30

This project was stitched over two on 28-count antique white Zweigart Jubilee. Two strands were used when stitching with the DMC floss, while only one strand was used when stitching with the Kreinik #8 Gold Braid.

cottage lane designs

84-715 Beaver Lake Road, Kelowna, British Columbia, Canada
V4V 1E6
250-766-1982
e-mail: Cottagelane@telus.net

Project Color Key

	DMC	ANCHOR	
◪	311	148	Navy Blue Medium
❖⊠	312	979	Baby Blue Very Dark
❖②	322	978	Baby Blue Dark
⊟	676	891	Old Gold Light
⌂	729	890	Old Gold Medium
■	939	152	Navy Blue Very Dark
⊟	3829	901	Old Gold Very Dark
❖↑	002 Gold Kreinik #8 Braid		
❖◪	Backstitch with one strand of DMC 869		

❖ 'Cross the Lilliebridge

Jennifer & Peter Lilliebridge

"WE'RE IN GOOD HANDS"

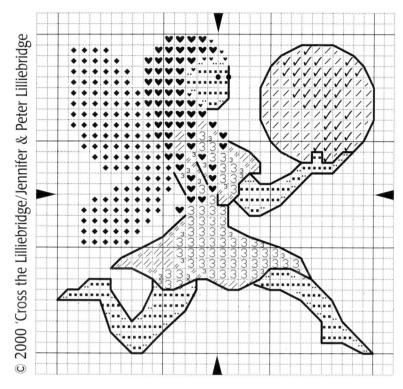

© 2000 'Cross the Lilliebridge/Jennifer & Peter Lilliebridge

Stitch Count: 30 x 30

This project was stitched over two threads on 28-count antique white Zweigart Cashel Linen. Two strands of DMC floss were used for all of the cross stitches, but in two cases, Kreinik 012 Blending Filament was added to the floss as indicated below by 012BF.

Several different colors were used in the backstitching as shown in the color chart below.

Project Color Key

	DMC	ANCHOR	
◪	334	977	Baby Blue Medium*
☑	367	217	Pistachio Green Dark**
◉	550	102	Violet Very Dark***
❖ ③	552	99	Violet Light + one strand of 012BF
❖ ◨	554	96	Violet Medium + one strand of 012BF
⊡	819	271	Baby Pink Light
♥	947	330	Burnt Orange

☑ Backstitch Fairy's dress with one strand of DMC 550/Anchor 102

☑ Backstitch Earth with one strand of Kreinik 006HL #8 Braid

❖ ☑ Backstitch Fairy's skin with one strand of DMC 899/Anchor 52

● French Knot with one strand of DMC 939/Anchor 152

*The sample shown here was actually stitched with DMC #30813 Rayon. **The sample shown here was actually stitched with DMC #30367 Rayon. ***The sample shown here was actually stitched with DMC #30550 Rayon.

'Cross the Lilliebridge™

P.O. Box 28214,
Spokane, Washington, 99228
e-mail: lilliebridge@mindspring.com
website: www.crossthelilliebridge.com

❖ *Desert Knight Enterprises, Inc.*

Sarah Givens

"HEART'S CELEBRATION"

Stitch Count: 60 x 60

This project was stitched over one on 28-count antique white Cashel Linen. Work all stitches with one strand of floss. Work all cross stitches first. Use one strand of Kreinik 032 Blending Filament with one strand of DMC 3072 for the needle. The backstitching around the heart is DMC 899, and the backstitching of the figure's thread is DMC 939.

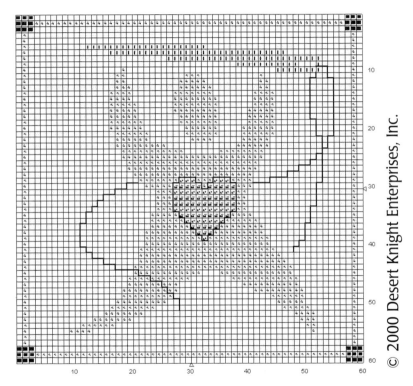

© 2000 Desert Knight Enterprises, Inc.

Project Color Key

	DMC	ANCHOR	
⌃	729	890	Old Gold - med
ⓐ	776	24	Pink - med
⊟	899	52	Rose - med
■	939	152	Navy Blue - vy dk
⏋	3072	847	Beaver Grey - vy lt

Desert Knight Enterprises, Inc.
380 Front St. S.
Issaquah, WA 98027
425-837-5310
e-mail: sgivens@mail.com

❖ Designs by Catherine Kronenwetter

Catherine Kronenwetter

"LABOR OF LOVE"

© 2000 Catherine Kronenwetter

Stitch Count: 30 x 30

This project was stitched over two on 28-count antique white Cashel Linen using two strands of floss. Full, half, and quarter stitches were each worked in two strands of floss.

Project Color Key

	DMC	ANCHOR	
⊠	311	148	Navy Blue-MD
▲	814	45	Garnet-DK
⊡	899	52	Rose-MD

Floss Used for Backstitches (use two strands):

	DMC	ANCHOR	
◪	311	148	Navy Blue-MD - Outline on 1/2 stitch heart
◪	814	45	Garnet-DK - Outline on small French Knot heart
◪	899	52	Rose-MD
◪	939	152	Navy Blue-VY DK - All lettering and two small hearts

Floss Used for French Knots:

	DMC	ANCHOR	
●	311	148	Navy Blue-MD - Larger heart w/o outline
●	814	45	Garnet-DK - Small heart w/outline
●	939	152	Navy Blue-VY DK - Dots on "i"s

Designs by Catherine Kronenwetter
2139 S. Fountain Ave.
Appleton, WI 54915
e-mail: clkronenwetter@cs.com
website:
www.catherinekronenwetter.com

❖ Dragon Dreams

Jennifer L. Aikman-Smith

"HERE BE DRAGONS"

Stitch Count: 30 x 30

This project was stitched over two on 28-count antique white Zweigart Jubilee. Two strands were used when stitching with the DMC floss, while only one strand was used when stitching with the Kreinik #4 Very Fine Braid.

© 2000 Dragon Dreams Inc.

Project Color Key

	DMC	ANCHOR	
r	368	214	Pistachio Green Light
N	500	683	Blue Green Very Dark
:	501	878	Blue Green Dark
M	502	877	Blue Green
+	504	1042	Blue Green Very Light
a	776	24	Pink Medium
◙	839	360	Beige Brown Dark
÷	899	52	Rose Medium
❖ G	002HL		Gold Kreinik #4 Very Fine Braid
❖ ⋈	011HL		Gun Metal Kreinik #4 Very Fine Braid
⁄	Backstitch with one strand of 310/403		
●	French Knot with one strand of 310/403		

112 Highmeadow Drive,
Moncton, New Brunswick, Canada
E1G 2C4
e-mail: dragondr@nbnet.nb.ca
website: DragonDreams.accra.ca

❖ Dragon Fire Designs

Sherry Schons

"BALLOON CELEBRATION"

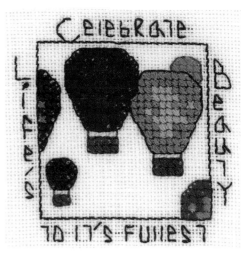

© 2000 Sherry Schons, Dragon Fire Designs

Stitch Count: 30 x 30

This project was stitched over two on antique white Cashel Linen using two strands of floss. One strand of floss was used for all of the backstitching. Please refer to the table below to see which objects are backstitched in what color.

Project Color Key

	DMC	ANCHOR	
⊗	309	42	Rose-DK
⊠	311	148	Navy Blue-MD
☑	367	217	Pistachio Grn-DK
H	498	1005	Christmas Red-DK
∅	740	316	Tangerine
▣	839	360	Beige Brown-DK
▣	890	218	Pistachio Grn-UL DK
▼	931	1034	Antique Blue-MD
V	932	1033	Antique Blue-LT
▼	947	330	Burnt Orange

Floss Used for French Knot:
●	890	218	Pistachio Grn-UL DK

Backstitching:

	DMC	ANCHOR	
☑	311	148	Navy Blue-MD - Navy Blue Balloon
☑	740	316	Tangerine
☑	814	45	Garnet-DK - red hot air balloon
☑	839	360	Beige Brown-DK - gondolas
☑	890	218	Pistachio Grn-UL DK - green hot air balloon, words, square of border
☑	947	330	Burnt Orange - orange balloons
☑	3750	1036	Antique Blue-VY DK - blue balloon

Dragon Fire Designs
3198 2nd St.
Marion, IA 52302
e-mail: rsakj@soli.inav.net

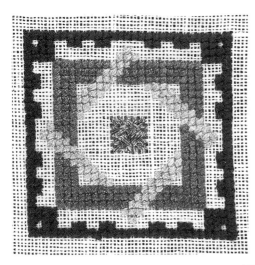

Duo Designs

Sandra S. Arthur
and Teresa Kinberger

"GRAPE WAFFLE"

Stitch Count: 30 x 30

This project was stitched on 28-count antique white Zweigart Cashel Linen. Use three strands of floss and complete the border and celtic square with cross stitch. The center motif is a Waffle Stitch stitched with Shimmer Ribbon Floss 148F 40.

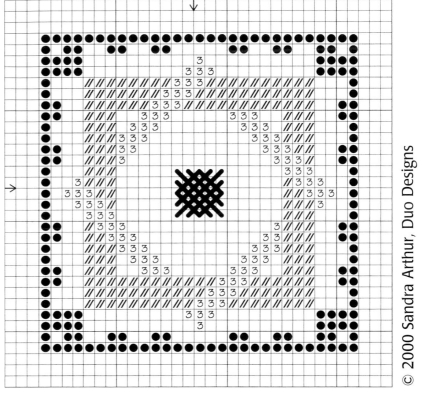

CROSS STITCH AND NEEDLEPOINT

325 Chilesburg Road
Lexington, KY 40509
859-264-9562
e-mail: ssa@concentric.net

Project Color Key

	DMC	ANCHOR	
◈	550	102	Violet - VY DK
3	552	99	Violet - MD
▨	554	96	Violet - LT

❖ Handy Links to Copyright Information

The Internet is a wonderful place to find more information about copyright issues, particularly because so many people involved in the digital field are wrestling with some of the same questions you may have. Here are links to some of the more helpful and informative sites about copyright.

A Brief Introduction to Copyright
www.templetons.com/brad/copyright.html

Ten Big Myths About Copyright
www.clari.net./brad/copymyths.html

The UT System Crash Course in Copyright
www.utsystem.edu/ogc/intellectualproperty/cprtindx.htm

Copyright and Fair Use
http://fairuse.stanford.edu/

Copyright Resources on the Internet
http://groton.k12.ct.us/mts/pt2a.htm

Copyright Website
www.benedict.com/contents.htm

Copyright Issues on the Web
www.aitech.ac.jp/~iteslj/Articles/Harris-Copyright.html

Copyright Clearance Center
www.copyright.com

U.S Copyright Office
http://lcweb.loc.gov./copyright/

Canadian Copyright Information
http://cipo.gc.ca

Australian Copyright Council
www.copyright.org.au/

European Copyright User Platform
www.eblida.org/ecup/

APIC- Association for the Protection of Internet Copyright
www.a-w.org/index.html

Faded Tapestries - Copyright & Artists on the Internet
www.dreamfires.com/tapestries/index.html

❖ Elegant Designs

Elizabeth Ann Angus

"ANGEL OF CELEBRATION"

Stitch Count: 30 x 30

This project was stitched over two on antique white Cashel Linen.

Row 1: Satin Stitch Design - Use one strand of #12 White Pearl Cotton.

Row 2: Double Leviathan Stitch - Use one strand of #12 - see stitch diagram (in the back of this book), do 13 complete stitches.

Row 3: Angel - Angel Wings are done with #12; fill in completely with a Smyrna Cross Stitch. Head - two little "x"s are the placement for her hair. The three little dots are Mill Hill Petite Beads 42018. Outline her dress with one strand of 369 and use two strands for her bouquet. Hair - one strand of 839. Face - one strand of 950. Checks - one strand of 758. Eyes - one strand of 839.

Row 4: Flowers - Use one strand of #12 to do Ribbed Spider Web. The stems are done with The Thread Gatherer Silk Ribbon - Willow Green. Use short pieces of ribbon. Bring your ribbon up, letting it form a little pleat, and be very careful not to let it twist. Take it down and to the back of the linen, bring it back up carefully to make the two little leaves, allowing it to make little pleats.

Elegant Designs
433 Valdapena Ct.
Escalon, CA 95320
209-838-7146

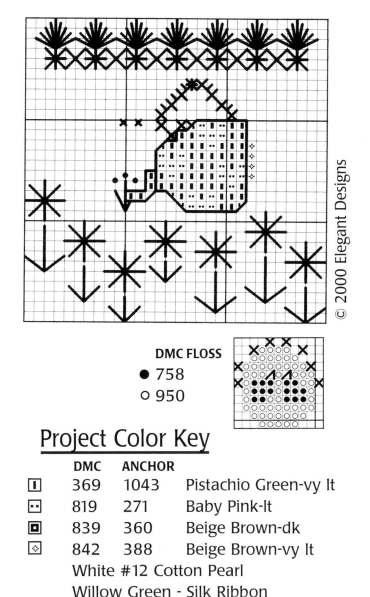

© 2000 Elegant Designs

DMC FLOSS

● 758
○ 950

Project Color Key

	DMC	ANCHOR	
▯	369	1043	Pistachio Green-vy lt
⊡	819	271	Baby Pink-lt
▣	839	360	Beige Brown-dk
⊗	842	388	Beige Brown-vy lt

White #12 Cotton Pearl

Willow Green - Silk Ribbon

42018 - Mill Hill Petite Beads

Silk Ribbon courtesy of The Thread Gatherer
DMC Floss courtesy of DMC Corp.

❖ Enchanting Lair

Laura Dickson

"SMALL BUT MIGHTY"

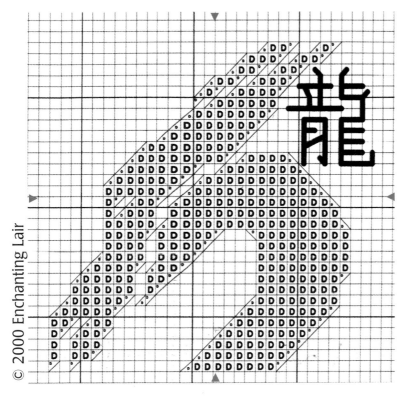

© 2000 Enchanting Lair

Stitch Count: 30 x 30

This project was stitched over two on 28-count antique white Zweigart Cashel Linen.

The dragon was stitched with one strand of floss and one strand of blending filament, while the back-stitching for the "dragon" symbol was done using two strands of DMC and one of blending filament.

The dragon in the model was stitched with Kreinik Peacock BF085. Blending Filament allows you to change the DMC floss color to any other you choose. This dragon could be black, grey, yellow, or blue—open your imagination and enjoy!

Project Color Key

	DMC	ANCHOR	
⊡	501	878	Blue Green Dark mixed with Blending Filament ❖

Enchanting Lair

P.O. Box 21108 Algonquin,
North Bay, Ontario, Canada
P1B 9N8
e-mail: laura@onlink.net
website: www.enchantinglair.com

Frances & Me

Deb Brewer

"BIRDHOUSE CELEBRATION"

Stitch Count: 26w x 25h

This project was stitched over two on 28-count antique white Zweigart Cashel Linen. Two strands of floss were used for the cross stitches, and only one strand of floss was used in the backstitching.

Embellish this birdhouse with the buttons of your choice. You can even use tiny butterflies or bumblebees instead of feathered friends!

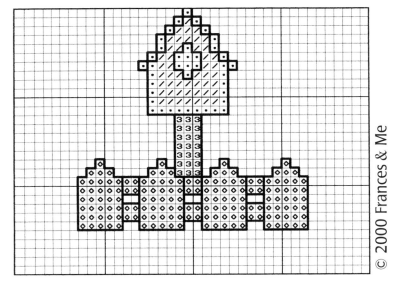

© 2000 Frances & Me

Project Color Key

	DMC	ANCHOR	
◉	550	102	Violet - vy dk
▣	552	99	Violet - med
◪	554	96	Violet - lt
◈	842	388	Beige Brown - vy lt

Floss Used for Backstitches:

◪	550	102	Violet - vy dk (birdhouse)
◪	841	378	Beige Brown - lt (fence)

Frances & Me
2729 Payne Rd.
Des Moines, IA 50310
e-mail: brewerdm@phibred.com

FulmerCraft

Cheri Fulmer

"CELEBRATE AMERICA'S NATIONAL PARKS"

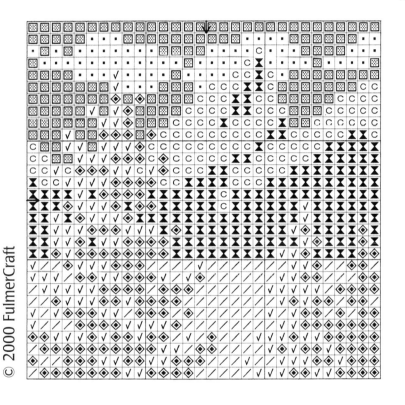

© 2000 FulmerCraft

Stitch Count: 30 x 30

This project was stitched over two on 28-count antique white Zweigart. Cross stitch using three strands of floss on your choice of either 14-count white Aida or over two threads on 28-count antique white Cashel Linen.

Project Color Key

	DMC	ANCHOR	
◪	334	977	Baby Blue - med
☑	367	217	Pistachio Green - dk
☒	646	8581	Beaver Grey - dk
C	648	900	Beaver Grey - lt
◈	890	218	Pistachio Green - ul dk
▨	3325	129	Baby Blue - lt
·	5200	1	Snow White

FulmerCraft/National Park Needlework
P.O. Box 34
Moose, WY 83012
e-mail:
nationalparkneedleart@rmisp.com

❖ *Golden Circle Designs*

G. Romilly Goodfellow

"LITTLE GRYPHON"

Stitch Count: 30 x 30

This project was stitched over two on antique white Cashel Linen.

1. Complete all cross stitches using two strands of floss.
2. Backstitch the talons with 3829 Old Gold - vy dk.
3. Backstitch the Gryphon and border with one strand of 939 Navy Blue - vy dk.
4. Work the French Knot eye with one strand of 939 Navy Blue - vy dk.
5. Work the large Algerian Eyelets with two strands of 552 Violet - md.
6. Work the outside ring of Algerian Eyelets with two strands of 309 Rose - dk.
7. Work the inside ring of the Algerian Eyelets with two strands of 552 Violet - md, except for the eyelet at each corner, which should be worked with two strands of 309 Rose - dk.

Golden CircleDesigns

10201 Lindley Ave. #F-90
Northridge, CA 91325
818-360-0394
e-mail: deromiffy@mindspring.com

Project Color Key

	DMC	ANCHOR	
◙	309	42	Rose - dk
③	552	99	Violet - md
⧄	554	96	Violet - lt
⊟	676	891	Old Gold - lt
⊼	729	890	Old Gold - md
L	743	302	Yellow - md
⊟	3829	901	Old Gold - vy dk

❖ *Graceful Lily Needlework*

Nancy Sue Havener

"BLACKWORK SPREE"

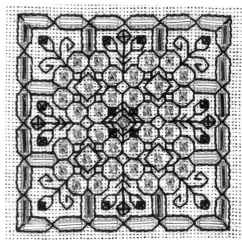

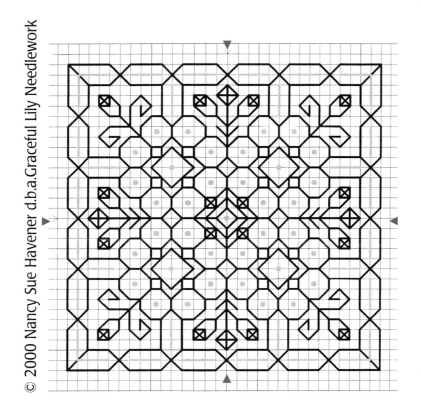

Stitch Count: 30 x 30

This project was stitched over two on 28-count antique white.

1. Stitch all dark lines using a single strand of DMC #939. Use a back-stitch or Double Running Stitch.

2. Before attaching the small bugle beads, examine all of the beads in the package. A few are probably slightly shorter than the others. Reserve these shorter beads to use in the corners.

3. Attach the small bugle beads using a single strand of DMC #739. Go through each bead twice.

4. Attach the seed beads using a double strand of DMC #739. Instead of going through the bead a second time, take another stitch, but split the thread so that one strand goes on each side of the bead. This will help set the bead and ensure it sits up straight.

Project Color Key

DMC	ANCHOR	
■ 939	152	Navy Blue - vy dk
—	Mill Hill Small Bugle Bead #72011	
•	Mill Hill Glass Seed Bead #02011	

GRACEFUL LILY
NEEDLEWORK

21431 Lake Shore Blvd.
Euclid, OH 44123
216-731-4751
e-mail: nshlily@aol.com

❖ Harbour Light Designs

Paula L. Towner

"SPRING HEART"

Stitch Count: 61 x 61

This project was stitched over two on 28-count antique white Zweigart Cashel Linen.

Step 1: Using one strand of Wildflower Meadow 003, stitch the outside border. They are straight stitches over four threads.

Step 2: Using one strand of #8 Perle Cotton 899, stitch the pulled Up-right Cross Stitch, starting at the top center. Remember to pull tight.

Step 3: Using one strand of Wildflower Meadow, stitch the Roman Cross variation square in the center.

Step 4: Using two strands of DMC floss 504, stitch the Four-way Continental Stitch between the Roman Cross and the Up-right Cross Stitch. Place a silver Mill Hill bead in the center of the Four-way Continental Stitches.

Step 5: Using two strands of DMC floss 501, stitch the Diagonal Mosaic Stitch in the corners.

Step 6: Using two strands of DMC floss 776, stitch the Double Straight Cross Stitch next to the Diagonal Mosaic Stitch.

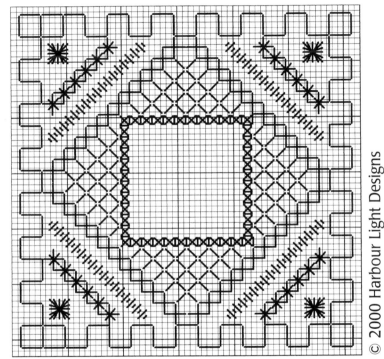

Step 7: Using two strands of DMC floss 501, stitch the Eyelet Stitch in the corners.

Step 8: Stitch the Heart treasure in the center with DMC floss 776 and add a bead in the center.

Harbour Light Designs
1830 W. Main St.
League City, Texas 77573
281-332-3039
e-mail: pltharbour@aol.com

Project Color Key

	DMC	ANCHOR	
⊡	501	878	Blue Green - DK
⊞	504	1042	Blue Green - VY LT
⊡	776	24	Pink - MD
❖	Wildflower Meadow 003		
❖	#8 Perle Cotton 899		
❖	Mill Hill Bead 42010 silver		
❖	Mill Hill Treasure 12067 pink heart		

❖Heartfelt Designs

Carol Stone

"CELTIC KNOT"

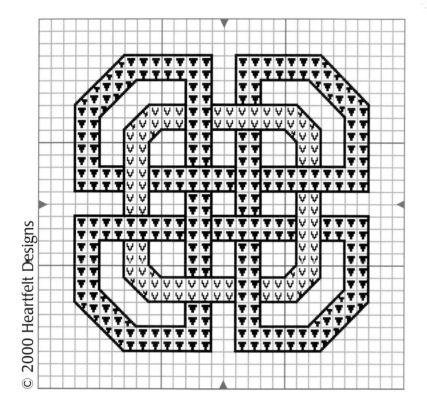

© 2000 Heartfelt Designs

Stitch Count: 30 x 30

This project was stitched over two on 28-count antique white Zweigart Jubilee. Two strands of regular DMC floss were used for the cross stitches and one strand of regular DMC floss for the backstitching.

Project Color Key

	DMC	ANCHOR	
▼	931	1034	Antique Blue light
ⱴ	932	1033	Antique Blue Medium
▨	3750	1036	Backstitch in one strand of Antique Blue Very Dark

Heartfelt Designs

59 Martinac Crescent,
Regina, Saskatchewan, Canada
S4X 1R5
e-mail: cstorie@accesscomm.ca
website: www.geocities.com/heartfeltdesigns

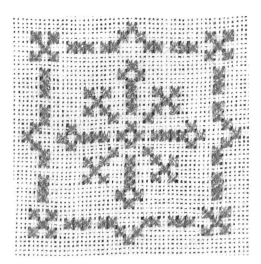

❖ *Holly House*

D. Elliott

"WINTER SNOWFLAKE"

Stitch Count: 24 x 24

This project was stitched on 28-count antique white Cashel Linen using two strands of DMC floss and one strand of Kreinik blending filament over two threads of fabric.

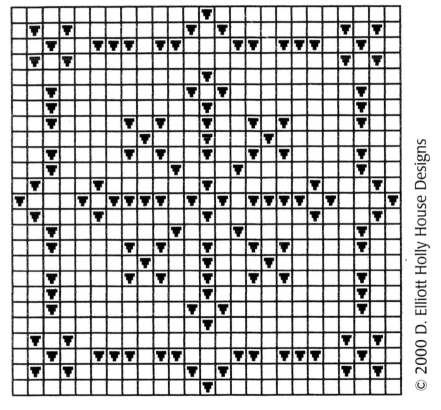

Project Color Key

	DMC	ANCHOR	
▼	931	1034	Antique Blue - MD
❖	Kreinik Blending Filament #032		

Holly House
e-mail: Hollyh32@aol.com

❖ *Illusions*

Vicky Graham

COPY

"EGYPTIAN SCARAB"

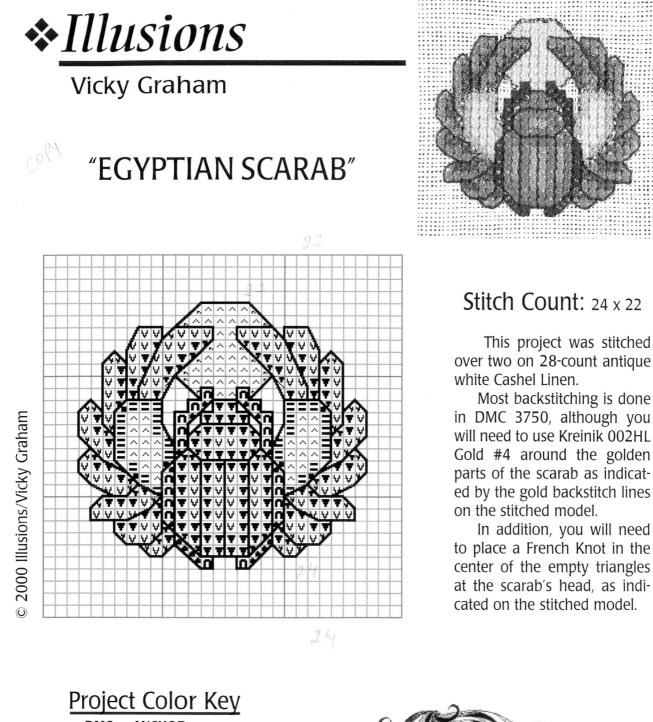

© 2000 Illusions/Vicky Graham

Stitch Count: 24 x 22

This project was stitched over two on 28-count antique white Cashel Linen.

Most backstitching is done in DMC 3750, although you will need to use Kreinik 002HL Gold #4 around the golden parts of the scarab as indicated by the gold backstitch lines on the stitched model.

In addition, you will need to place a French Knot in the center of the empty triangles at the scarab's head, as indicated on the stitched model.

Project Color Key

	DMC	ANCHOR	
⌃	729	890	Old Gold - med
▼	931	1034	Antique Blue - med
⊻	932	1033	Antique Blue - lt
⋂	3750	1036	Antique Blue - vy dk
⊟	3829	901	Old Gold - vy dk
❖ ▨	Kreinik 002HL Gold #4 VFB		

P.O. Box 181
Grafton, WI 53024
262-375-8792

❖ *Imaginating Inc.*

Diane Arthurs

"HEAVENLY HANNAH"

Stitch Count: 30 x 30

This project was stitched over two on 28-count antique white Zweigart Jubliee. Two strands of floss were used for the cross stitches, and one strand of floss was used in the backstitching, as indicated below.

This design may be embellished with a tiny star, as shown, or with a charm of your choice.

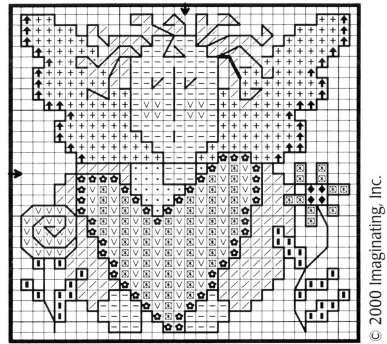

Project Color Key

	DMC	ANCHOR	
⊠	309	42	Rose - deep
↑	334	977	Baby Blue - med
/	729	890	Old Gold - med
∨	776	24	Pink - med
✿	814	45	Garnet - dk
−	819	271	Baby Pink - lt
◆	844	1041	Beaver Grey - ul dk
▮	890	218	Pistachio Green - ul dk
+	3325	129	Baby Blue - lt
·	5200	1	Snow White

Floss used for Backstitches (one strand):
☑ Leaves and stems - 890 - Pistachio Green - ul dk
☑ All other backstitches - 844 - Beaver Grey - ul dk

Imaginating Inc.
P.O. Box 156
Rootstown, OH 44272
e-mail: imag8ing@aol.com
website: www. imaginating.com

❖ *In A Gentle Fashion*

Linda Palmer

"IN A GENTLE FASHION"

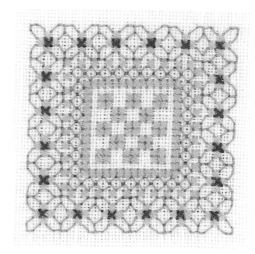

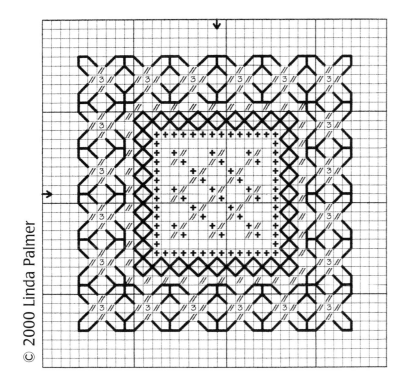

© 2000 Linda Palmer

Stitch Count: 30 x 30

This project was stitched over two on 28-count antique white Cashel Linen. Cross stitches should be completed using two strands of floss. One strand of floss was used for all of the backstitching. Each square of the chart equals two threads.

Project Color Key

	DMC	ANCHOR	
+	504	1042	Vy Lt. Blue Green
3	552	99	Med. Violet
⁄	554	96	Lt. Violet
⁄	502	877	All backstitches

In A Gentle Fashion
14451 W. Calla Rd.
Salem, OH 44460
1-800-7STITCH
e-mail: iagfpalmer@juno.com

❖Intostitch Designs

Kim Howe

"THIS IS AUSTRALIA"

Stitch Count: 28 x 28

This project was stitched on 28-count antique white Cashel Linen using two strands of floss or one strand of rayon as indicated.

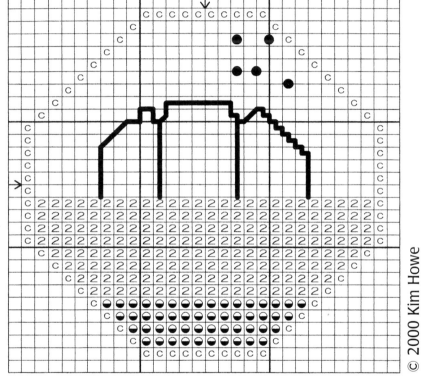

© 2000 Kim Howe

Project Color Key

	DMC	ANCHOR	
c	729	890	Stranded Cotton (two strands)
◒	890	218	Stranded Cotton (two strands)
2	976		Rayon (one strand)

Satin Stitch (two strands) Sampler Threads Terracotta
Satin Stitch on angle (left to right) between the lines.
Mill Hill Petite Beads:
42028 (Small star in Southern Cross)
03038 (Large stars in Southern Cross)
Attach beads with one strand of Terracotta

Intostitch Designs
41 Network Dr.
Wynnum West Qld 4178
Australia
61-7-3396-9359
e-mail: pknahowe@optusnet.com.au

 **It's A Stitch!**

Cindy Brown

"HARDANGER SQUARE"

© 2000 It's A Stitch

Stitch Count: 30 x 30

This project was stitched over two on 28-count antique white Cashel linen.

Stitch the modified Blanket Stitch edging around the perimeter of the design using one strand of Caron Wildflowers #005.

Stitch the kloster blocks and modified klosters using DMC #8 Perle Cotton #554.

Cut and remove threads inside the kloster blocks as shown in the chart. Although it appears on the chart that five threads have been removed at each kloster block, in fact only four threads should be removed, leaving four thread groups between the removed threads. This was done for the sake of clarity on the Lacy Daisy weaving.

Needleweave the remaining threads inside the cut-out area. The weaving is done over four threads in spite of the way it looks in the diagrams in the back of this book.

Using Kreinik 1/8 Ribbon 012HL, weave the Lacy Daisy figure over the top of the needlewoven bars. You will need to use an 18-inch piece of ribbon for this, because there is no easy way of ending and beginning a new piece. When weaving the ribbon, do not start by attaching the ribbon, not even with a waste knot because this will get in the way. Just leave about a 3-inch tail, and try to hold it in place until you complete several wraps. You will anchor it under the weaves when the figure is completed. Follow the diagrams carefully for the weaving and try not to twist the ribbon. When the weaving is completed, finish the ends off by weaving them under the ribbon near the center of flower.

The weaving is shown in closer detail in the diagrams in the back of this book in two different colors on line styles. The green lines indicate weaving done in a counterclockwise direction. Begin at the arrow and weave all the way around. When you get back to the arrow, reverse directions and follow the orange line.

Project Color Key

❖ Caron Wildflowers #005 Sky Blue Pink (modified buttonhole edge)
❖ DMC #8 Perle Cotton #554 (kloster blocks and needlewoven bars)
❖ Kreinik 1/8 Ribbon 012HL* (Lacy Daisy weaving)

*If you would prefer a less dense look to the flower, use Kreinik 1/16 Ribbon.

It's A Stitch!
35 Woodland Rd.
Pittsford, NY 14534
e-mail: cpbrown48@aol.com
website: http://itsastitch.homesteadcom/index.html

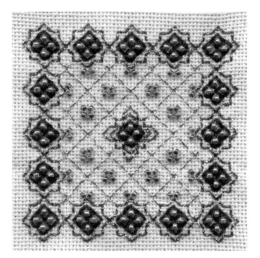

Jazzbird Designs

Catherine Lawhon

"CELEBRATION"

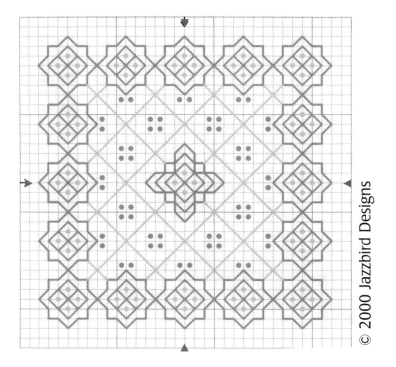

© 2000 Jazzbird Designs

Stitch Count: 30 x 30

This project was stitched over two on 28-count antique white Zweigart Jubilee. The stitches in this piece are all straight stitches. They can be executed as backstitches or Double Running Stitches, or a combination of the two. All stitches are to be worked over two threads at a time only, whether they are vertical, horizontal, or diagonal Each square on the graph represents two threads of the fabric.

Step 1: Using four strands of Kreinik #042 Blending Filament, stich the motifs indicated by the solid lines on the graph.

Step 2: Using two strands of DMC Rayon #30550, add the stitches indicated by the dotted lines, forming the clusters of four small diamonds.

Step 3: Using two strands of Kreinik Blending filament, Color #028, complete the stitches indicated by the dashed lines.

Step 4: Using a single strand of sewing thread matching the fabric color, sew Mill Hill Petite Beads onto the fabric with one half cross. Color #40557 will be used inside the small purple diamonds. Color #40252 will be used inside the large gold diamonds.

Project Color Key

- ❖ Kreinik 042 Blending Filament
- ❖ DMC Purple Rayon 30550
- ❖ Kreinik 028 Blending Filament
- ❖ Mill Hill Petite Beads 40557
- ❖ Mill Hill Petite Beads 40252

Jazzbird Designs
1633 Itchepackesassa Dr.
Lakeland, FL 33810-0161

❖ *Leon Conrad Designs*

Leon Conrad

"PATCHWORK N' BLACKWORK"

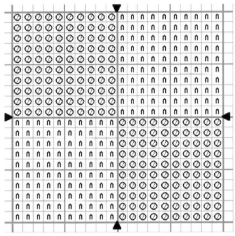

Fig. 1

Stitch Count: 40 x 40

This project was stitched over one on 28-count antique white Zweigart Cashel Linen.

1. For the best results, mount your fabric on a slate frame. Stitch the four background squares as shown in Fig. 1 in Basketweave Tent Stitch using two strands of DMC stranded cotton. Each square measures 20 x 20 stitches over one thread.

2. Following the chart in Fig. 2, stitch the red and blue outlines in Double Running Stitch using one strand of DMC, working over two threads. Leave the spaces marked 1, 2, 3, 4 in Fig. 2 unfilled. Work the black lines shown in Fig. 2 in Straight Stitches using one strand of white DMC, taking long stitches and maintaining an even tension and positioning your stitches carefully.

Fig. 2

Fig. 3

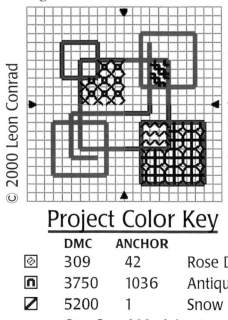

© 2000 Leon Conrad

3. Stitch the blackwork filling patterns shown as black lines in Fig. 3 in the spaces which remain unfilled in your design in Running Back Stitch using as small a needle as possible threaded with one strand Maderia Aerofil - White. The completed design is shown at the top of the page.

4. Remove your work from the frame. Iron/Press if necessary and make into an elegant scissor fob using trimmings of your choice.

Project Color Key

	DMC	ANCHOR	
⊗	309	42	Rose Deep
n	3750	1036	Antique Blue Very Dark
◪	5200	1	Snow White (Fig. 2 only)
❖	One Spool Madeira Aerofil - White		

Leon Conrad Designs
20 Courtenay Street, Kennington,
London, UK SE11 5PQ
Tel +44 (0)20 7582 8213
e-mail: info@lcdesigns.org
website: www.lcdesigns.org

A Celebration of Stitching

41

❖ *Lesa Steele Designs*

Lesa Steele

"BLUE ICE"

Stitch Count: 30 x 30

This project was stitched on 28-count antique white Cashel. Cross stitch using two strands of floss. Use one strand/ply for all other stitches. Pull four-sided stitches and eyelets firmly to create a lacy effect. The finished design area measures 1-1/8 inches square at 28-count.

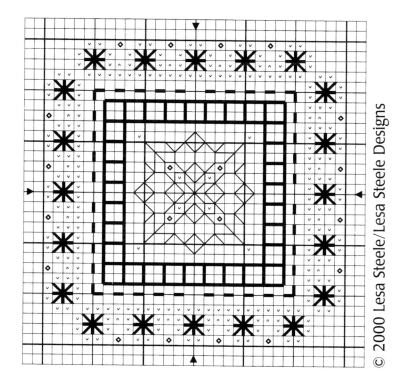

Project Color Key

	DMC	ANCHOR	
v	932	1033	Antique Blue lt
n	3750	1036	Antique Blue vy dk
Backstitches:			
⧄	3750	1036	Antique Blue vy dk (center motif)
❖ ⧄	032		Kreinik #4 Braid (check model)
❖ ⧄	932	1033	Antique Blue lt DMC Pearl Cotton No. 12 (check model)

❖ Mill Hill Crystal Seed Beads 00161

Lesa Steele Designs
18 Livingston Ct.
East Brunswick, NJ 00816
e-mail: info@lesasteeledesigns.com
website: www. lesasteeledesigns.com

Roses and Bluebells
Anne Brinkley Designs
Page 9

Celebration Butterfly
Another Time Designs
Page 10

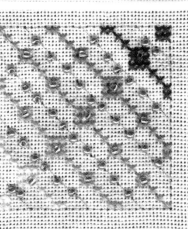

Flight of Fancy
Black Swan Designs
Page 11

Simply Elegant
Bunny Tales Cross Stitch Design
Page 12

Celtic Knot
Carolina Country House
Page 13

A Celebration of Stitching
Cat's Cradle Needleworks
Page 14

A Celebration of Stitching
Page 15

Celestial Miniature
Cottage Lane Designs
Page 16

We're in Good Hands
'Cross the Lilliebridge
Page 17

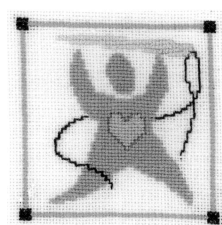

Heart's Celebration
Desert Knight Enterprises, Inc.
Page 18

Labor of Love
Designs by Catherine Kronenwetter
Page 19

Here Be Dragons
Dragon Dreams
Page 20

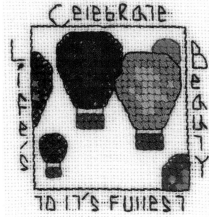

Balloon Celebration
Dragon Fire Designs
Page 21

Grape Waffle
Duo Designs
Page 22

Angel of Celebration
Elegant Designs
Page 24

Small But Mighty
Enchanting Lair
Page 25

Polar Bear with Northern Lights
Euphemia Forest Design
Page 26

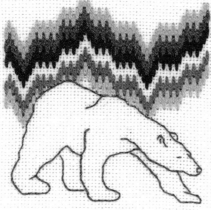

Days of Yore
Fanta Cat Designs
Page 27

Celebration Birdhouse
Frances & Me
Page 28

Celebrate America's National Parks
FulmerCraft
Page 29

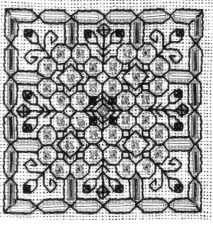

Little Gryphon
Golden Circle Designs
Page 30

Blackwork Spree
Graceful Lily Needlework
Page 31

Spring Heart
Harbour Light Designs
Page 32

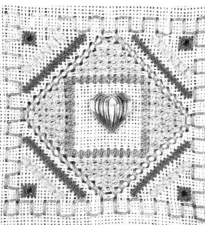

Celtic Knot
Heartfelt Designs
Page 33

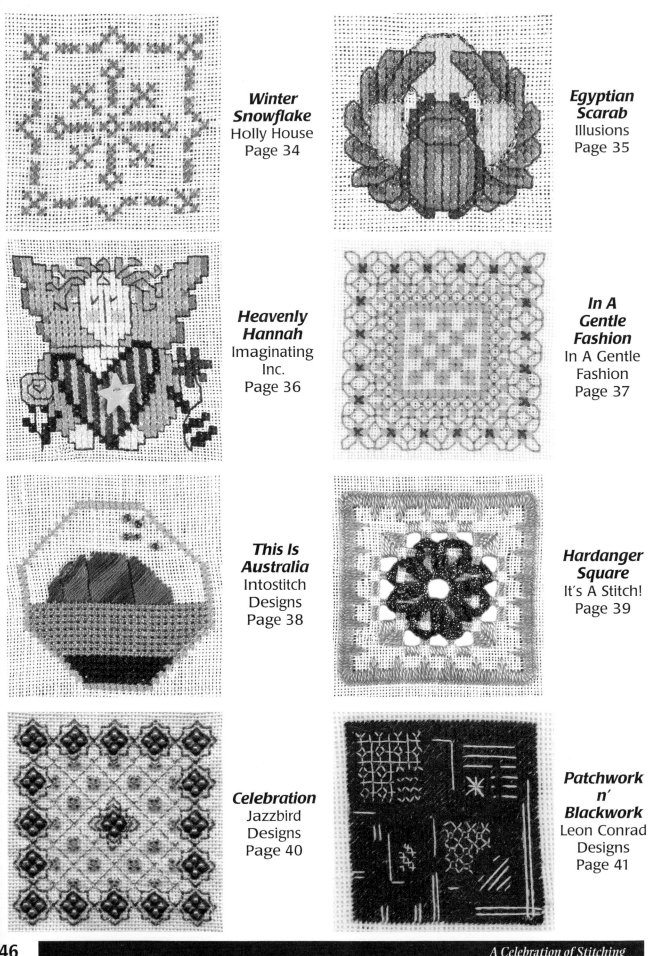

**Winter
Snowflake**
Holly House
Page 34

**Egyptian
Scarab**
Illusions
Page 35

**Heavenly
Hannah**
Imaginating
Inc.
Page 36

**In A
Gentle
Fashion**
In A Gentle
Fashion
Page 37

**This Is
Australia**
Intostitch
Designs
Page 38

**Hardanger
Square**
It's A Stitch!
Page 39

Celebration
Jazzbird
Designs
Page 40

**Patchwork
n'
Blackwork**
Leon Conrad
Designs
Page 41

Blue Ice
Lesa Steele
Designs
Page 42

Cherry Sky
Lisa
Overduin
Designs
Page 52

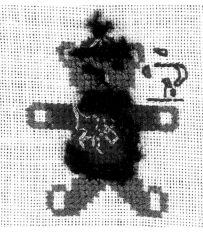

**Chinese
Bear**
Little
Treasures
Page 53

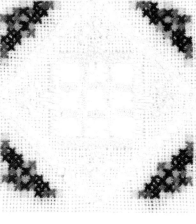

**Celebrate
Openwork**
Liz Navickas
Designs
Page 54

**Bless
the
Stitcher**
Lizzie*Kate
Page 55

Celebrate
Luminosity
Designs
Page 56

**Small
Seasons**
Marilyn and
Jackie's ...
Collectibles
Page 57

**Waterlily
Mother
and
Child**
Marnic
Designs
Page 58

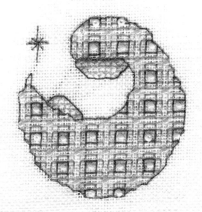

**Life's
Twinkles**
Meri's Motifs
Page 59

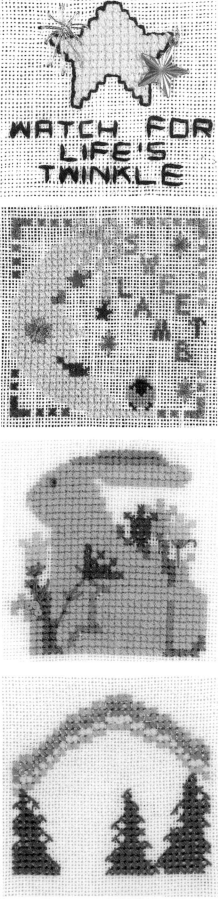

**Sweet
Lamb**
Moon Pi
Madness
Page 61

**Enjoying
the View**
Mosey 'n
Me
Page 63

**Rainbow
Over the
Pines**
Northern
Pine Designs
Page 65

Stained Glass Butterfly
Paw Prints
Cross Stitch
Page 67

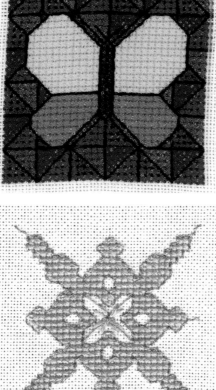

The Jade Turtle
Purrfect Spots
Page 68

Star Crystal
Risslee
Designs
Page 69

A Spring Basket
Sekas & Co.
Page 70

Mornin' All
Something In Common
Designs
Page 71

Infinite Love
Spirit of Design
Page 72

Mini Band Sampler
Stitchin'
Station
Page 73

Yesterday, Today & Tomorrow
Teixeira
Page 74

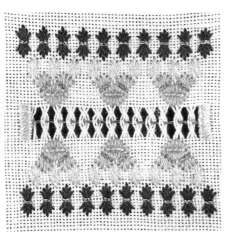

Royal Glory
Textured Treasures
Page 75

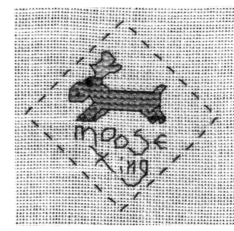

Moose Xing
The Stitcher's Habit
Page 76

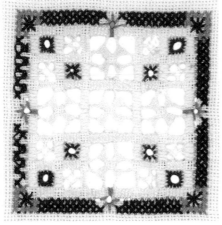

Hardanger Square
Threads of Grace
Page 78

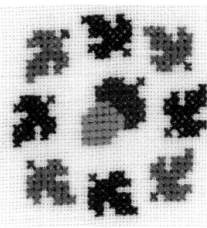

Autumn Acorn
Tink Boord-Dill Needlework
Page 79

Shalom: Peace to All
TovArt Designs
Page 80

Scarecrow Friend
Treasured Tapestries
Page 81

Flowers For A Friend
Twisted Threads
Page 82

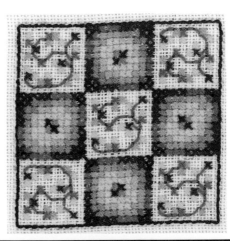

Wild Roses Quilt Square
Ursula Michael Designs
Page 83

**Spring
Bird**
Vickery
Collection
Page 84

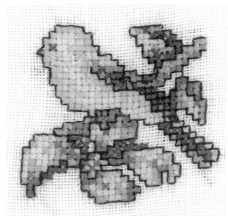

**Love to
Stitch**
Web Stitch
Page 85

**Sacred
Ankh**
Witches
Stitches
Page 86

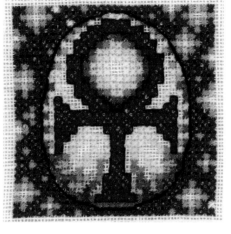

**Rose
Wreath**
Wren Song
Designs
Page 87

Chickadee
X's & Oh's
Page 88

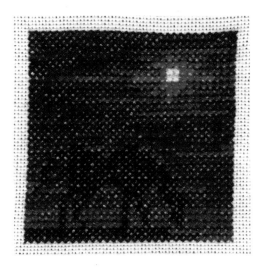

❖ *Lisa Overduin Designs*

Lisa Overduin

"CHERRY SKY"

Stitch Count: 30 x 30

This project was stitched over two on 28-count antique white Zweigart Jubilee. Two strands of DMC floss were used for all of the cross stitching.

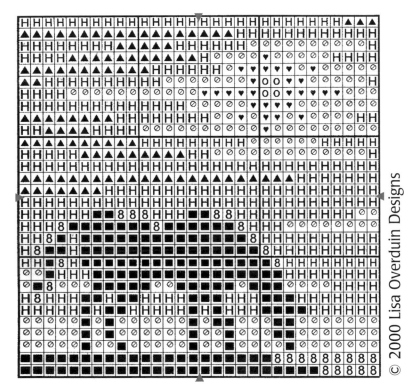

Project Color Key

	DMC	ANCHOR	
⊠	309	42	Rose - deep
⊠	311	148	Navy Blue - med
H	498	1005	Christmas Red - dk
▲	814	45	Garnet - dk
■	939	152	Navy Blue - vy dk
♥	947	330	Burnt orange
⊡	3823	386	Ultra pale yellow

Lisa Overduin Designs
1633 Dorion Avenue,
Ottawa, ON, Canada, K1G 0J7
e-mail: lisajoe@icons.net
website: www.icons.net/~lisajoe/

❖ *Little Treasures*

Charlotte C. Haas

"CHINESE BEAR"

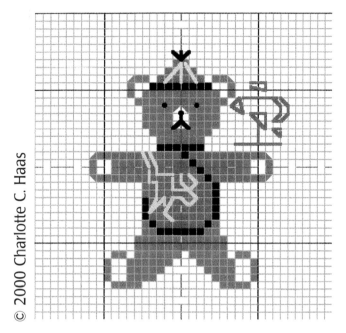

© 2000 Charlotte C. Haas

Starting from the front of the fabric, leave a tail, down at one, up at two, down at one, up at four, down at three, up at four, down at five, etc. Lock the thread in place on the diagonals, leaving your loops on the verticals to be trimmed and shaped at the end. If desired, and using a finer thread than the DMC Merino, the process can be repeated in reverse, crossing the Half Stitches. Clip all your loops and brush to fluff. Finish as desired.

Stitch Count: 26w x 31h

This little bear is all set to celebrate the Chinese New Year. The character says "little treasures." He's dedicated to Meridith Grace (Jiang YuCai) who came home to her Mommy and Daddy in October of 2000, the Year of the Dragon.

I've worked him in Dark Christmas Red (498) and Beige Brown (839), but he can be any color bear. Experiment with making him a little panda!

The "fur" trim of his coat is DMC Merino Noir, and the gold embroidery is DMC Metallic 5284.

Backstitching on the bear's face is done with one strand of DMC Merino Noir. The dragon on the coat and the backstitching on the hat are done with two strands DMC Metallic 5284.

Work all other stitches, including backstitching, before working the trim.

Anchor three loops of black at the top of his had with a French Knot for a "pom pom." Trim and brush to fluff.

His fur trim is Turkey Stitch, a half cross stitch done from the front side rather than the back (sort of).

```
 /|2  /|4
 /  |  /  |
1/  3 |/   |5
```

Project Color Key

DMC	ANCHOR	
⊞ 498	1005	Christmas Red - dk
▣ 839	360	Beige Brown - dk
❖ DMC Merino Noir		
❖ 5284 DMC Metallic		

Little Treasures
P.O. Box 181
Grafton, WI 53024
262-375-8792
e-mail: mammabunny@
thewamen.mil.wi.us

❖ *Liz Navickas Designs*

Liz Navickas

"CELEBRATE OPENWORK"

Stitch Count: 30 x 30

Each square on the graph equals two linen threads. Satin Stitch around the square of the hardanger design with white Perle cotton #8. Stitch joined eyelets with white Perle cotton #12. Stitch Reverse Double Faggot Stitch with white Perle cotton #12. This is shown on the chart as two solid lines with a dashed line between them. Cross stitch floral motifs with two strands of floss according to the chart. Cut and remove threads within the hardanger area as shown. Weave the bars completing a dove's eye where shown on chart with Perle cotton #12.

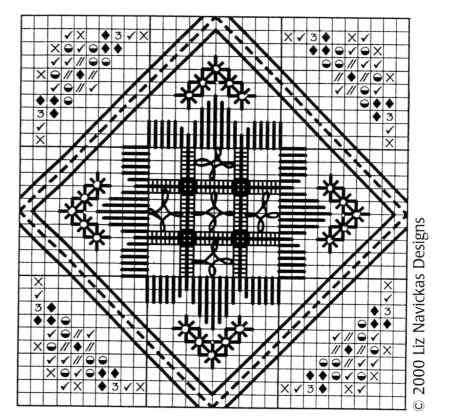

Liz Navickas Designs
RR #2 Box 2109
Hallstead, PA 18822
e-mail: navickas@epix.net
website:
www.members.spree.com/threats/
LizNDesigns

Project Color Key

	DMC	ANCHOR	
☑	367	217	Pistachio Green - dk
⬙	550	102	Violet - vy dk
3	552	99	Violet - med
▨	554	96	Violet - lt
⊠	744	301	Yellow - pale
⊜	890	218	Pistachio Green - ul dk

❖ *Lizzie*Kate*

Linda Ebright

"BLESS THE STITCHER"

© 2000 Lizzie*Kate, Inc.

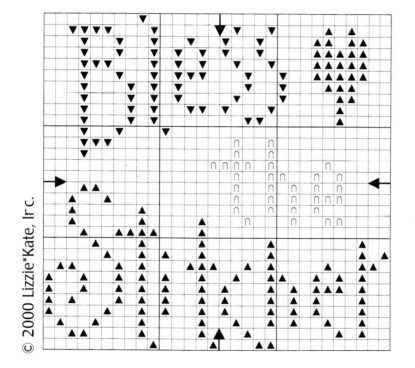

Stitch Count: 30 x 30

This project was stitched over two on 28-count antique white Cashel linen using two strands of floss.

Project Color Key

	DMC	ANCHOR	
▲	814	45	Garnet - dk
▼	931	1034	Antique Blue - med
⋒	3750	1036	Antique Blue - vy dk

Lizzie ☆ Kate

2901 Oriole
Wichita, KS 67204
316-832-0501
website: www.lizziekate.com

❖ *Luminosity Designs*

Jennifer Gilligan

"CELEBRATE"

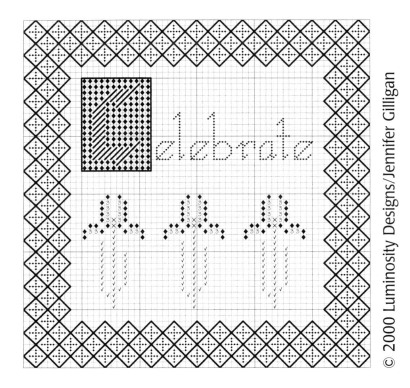

Stitch Count: 60 x 60

This project was stitched over one on 28-count antique white Cashel Linen.

1. The lattice work border is backstitched over two threads. Each square still represents one thread, but the stitches are two threads long.

2. The upright crosses in the border are also backstitched over two threads. The vertical stitch is made first and the horizontal stitch is made second.

3. The letter "C" is stitched using a Satin Stitch.

4. The border around the letter "C" is stitched with straight stitches.

5. The letters "elebrate" are backstitched over one thread. Each stitch is one thread long.

Luminosity Designs
13209 Windy Leaf Ct.
Woodbridge, VA 22192
e-mail: luminositydesign@home.com
website:
members.home.net/luminositydesign

Project Color Key

	DMC	ANCHOR	
☑	367	217	Pistachio Green - dk
◉	550	102	Violet - vy dk
③	552	99	Violet - med
☒	744	301	Yellow - pale

Backstitches:

550	102	Violet - vy dk
Kreinik 202HL		Aztec Gold #4 Braid

❖ *Marilynn and Jackie's... Collectibles*

Marilynn and Jackie Meyers

"SMALL SEASONS"

Stitch Count: 60 x 60

This project was stitched over one on 28-count white Cashel Linen using one strand of floss for the cross stitch. The final stitched size is 2-1/4 inches square.

Project Color Key

	DMC	ANCHOR	
✓	334	977	Baby Blue - med
✓	367	217	Pistachio Green - dk
⌐	368	214	Pistachio Green - lt
C	648	900	Beaver Grey - lt
L	743	302	Yellow - med
⋯	819	271	Baby Pink
◙	839	360	Beige Brown - dk
÷	899	52	Rose - med
■	939	152	Navy Blue - vy dk
♥	947	330	Burnt Orange

	DMC	ANCHOR	
⊡	3031	360	Mocha Brown - vy dk
⋔	3750	1036	Antique Blue - vy dk
⌁	3753	1031	Antique Blue - ultra vy lt
▣	3823	386	Old Gold - vy lt
⊡	5200	1	Snow White

Marilynn and Jackie's... Collectibles
P.O. Box 7065
Menlo Park, CA 94026
Phone/Fax 650-345-5844
e-mail: jackiemey@aol.com

Maria E. Cipp

"WATERLILY MOTHER AND CHILD"

Stitch Count: 30 x 30

This project was stitched over two on Wichelt's 28-count antique white Linen. This design celebrates the eternal love that a mother has for her child. The color selection is inspired by Monet's *Waterlily Pond,* painted in 1899.

Begin by cross stitching the faces with two strands of the DMC pinks. Then do the circular outline and star with the DMC metallic. Next, complete the blackwork by color backstitching with one strand of the dark green, light green, and blue as shown. Finally, attach the beads as indicated by their symbols in the blank spaces left between the blackwork.

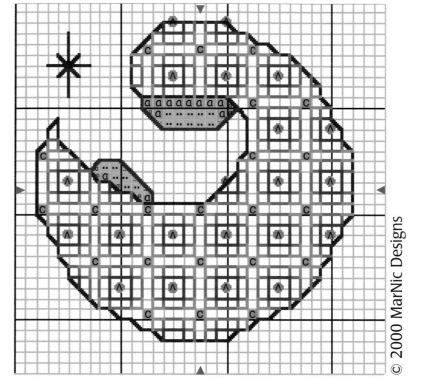

© 2000 MarNic Designs

Marnic Designs
692B Highpoint Ave.,
Waterloo, ON, Canada,
N2V 1G9
e-mail: marnicdesign@bond.net
website: www.bond/~marnicdesign/

Project Color Key

	DMC	ANCHOR	
☑	334	977	Baby Blue Medium
☑	368	214	Pistachio Green Light
a	776	24	Pink Medium
⊡	819	271	Baby Pink Light
☑	890	218	Pistachio Green Ultra Dark
☑	3031	360	Mocha Brown Dark
❖ ☑			Backstitch the star and circle outline of Mother and child in one strand of DMC blue Metallic 5291
❖ c			Mill Hill 00148 Yellow Bead
❖ ⋀			Mill Hill 00479 White Bead

❖ *Meri's Motifs*

Meridel Abrams

"LIFE'S TWINKLES"

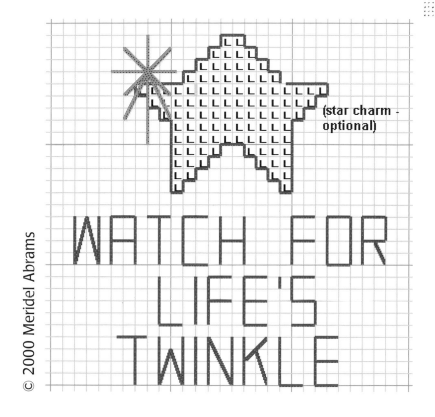

(star charm - optional)

© 2000 Meridel Abrams

Stitch Count: 26 x 29

This project can be stitched over 28-count antique white Cashel Linen or 28-count antique white Jubilee.

Optional: Attach a small gold star charm to one side of the star.

Project Color Key

	DMC	ANCHOR	
L	743	302	Yellow - med
■	939	152	Navy Blue - vy dk

The little twinkling star can be stitched with DMC 3829 Old Gold or with Kreinik's Gold Japan thread.

Meri's Motifs
website: www.themestream.com/articles/177706.htm

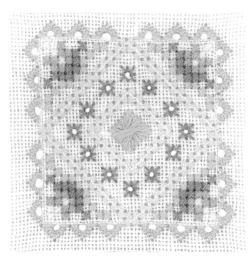

Kathleen O. Cadilek

"CELEBRATION OF STITCHING"

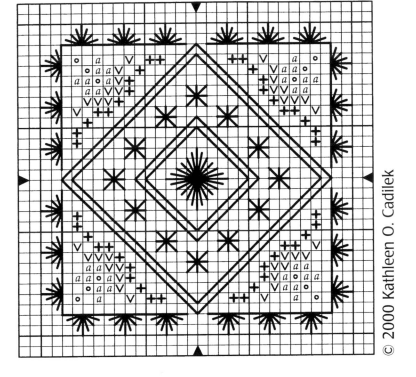

Stitch Count: 30 x 30

This project was stitched over two on 28-count antique white Zweigart Cashel Linen. Work the Diamond Rhodes first using two strands of the #504 floss. Use one strand of #819 pearl cotton to work the Cable Stitches. Use two strands of #932 floss to work the Algerian Eyelets. These stitches need to be pulled tightly to create a hole in the center. Work the cross stitches using two strands of floss in the color indicated. The Half Diamond Eyelets are worked with one strand of #3753 pearl cotton. These stitches need to be pulled tightly to create a hole in the center. Refer to the stitch diagrams at the back of this book for all specialty stitches. Each square represents two fabric threads.

The MonkeyWorks
5 Wychwood Lane
Oxford, CT 06478
203-888-1939
e-mail: k.cadilekgatt.net

Project Color Key

	DMC	ANCHOR	
+	504	1042	Blue Green - vy dk
a	776	24	Pink - med
❖ ⊡	819		#8 pearl cotton
V	932	1033	Antique Blue - lt
❖ ⌒	3753		#8 pearl cotton
□	3823	386	Ultra Pale Yellow

Each line represents one fabric thread.

❖ *Moon Pi Madness*

Merry Kathryn Mendenhall

"SWEET LAMB"

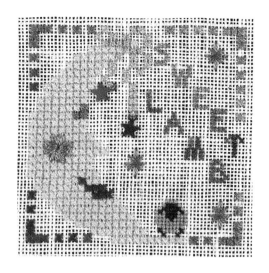

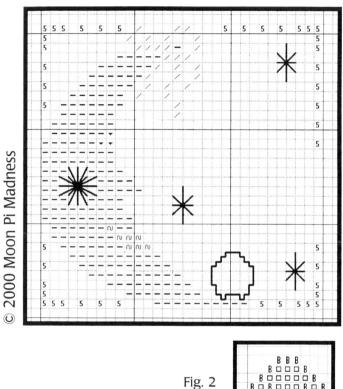

© 2000 Moon Pi Madness

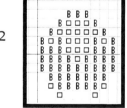

Fig. 2

Stitch Count: 58 x 59

This project was stitched over 28-count antique white Cashel Linen.

Use two strands when stitching over two fabric threads. Use one strand when stitching over one fabric thread. Stitch the moon's cheek in a modified Algerian Eyelet using two strands of 899 (do not pull).

Stitch the stars in a modified Smyrna cross using two strands of 931. Embellish with brass stars from Homespun Elegance.

Stitch the words as charted (Fig. 1). One grid represents one fabric thread. Stitch star and border from the master chart. They are only shown here to assist in placement.

Stitch the lamb as charted (Fig. 2). One grid represents one fabric thread.

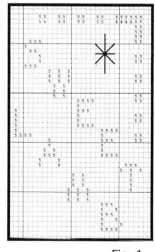

Fig. 1

Project Color Key

	DMC	ANCHOR	
2	309	42	Rose - deep
/	544		
—	676	891	Old Gold - lt
☐	839	360	Beige Brown - dk
B	841	378	Beige Brown - lt
	899	52	Rose - med
▼	931	1034	Antique Blue - med

❖ The Thread Gatherer - Silk 'n Colors
5 SNC 029 (Grape Melange)

411 Olustee Ave.
Lake City, FL 32025
904-752-0430
MoonPiMadness@aol.com

❖ *Moonshadow Stitchery*

Kristin Gulling-Smith

"MARDI GRAS"

Stitch Count: 60 x 60

This project was stitched over one on 28-count antique white Zweigart Jubilee. Each square on the chart represents one thread of the fabric. Start stitching from the center and work your way out.

1. Find the center of your fabric.

2. Work the Diamond Rhodes Stitch over 10 threads using two strands of 729.

3. Work the two diamond-shaped lines in Double Running Stitch using one strand of 550.

4. Stitch the Diamond Eyelets over six threads using two strands of 368, pulling each leg.

5. Stitch the vertical straight stitches in the diamond border over two threads, using two strands of 552.

6. Work the horizontal straight stitches in the diamond border over two threads in two strands of 368.

7. Work the Star Stitches over four threads in two strands of 554.

8. Stitch the cross stitch square over two threads using two strands of 729.

9. Stitch the outer diamond border in diagonal Satin Stitch using two strands of 550.

10. Work the Square Rhodes Stitches at the corners over seven threads using two strands of 552.

11. Work the Rice Stitches over five threads using two strands of 554.

12. Stitch the Star Stitches over four threads using two strands of 368.

13. Work the outer border in woven cross stitch over four threads using two strands of 367.

Moonshadow Stitchery
208 Prickett Ln. #2
Billings, MT 59101
e-mail: msstitchery:email.com
website:
www.crosswinds.net/~msstitchery/

Project Color Key

DMC	ANCHOR	
367	217	Pistachio Green - Dark
368	214	Pistachio Green - Light
550	102	Violet - Very Dark
552	99	Violet - Medium
554	96	Violet - Light
729	890	Old Gold - Medium

❖ *Mosey 'n Me*

Frank and Judy Bielec

"ENJOYING THE VIEW"

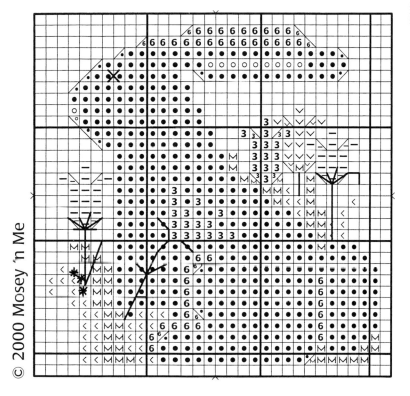

© 2000 Mosey 'n Me

Stitch Count: 30 x 30

This project was stitched over two on 28-count antique white Cashel Linen. The final size of the piece is 2 x 2 inches. This is a small stitching piece you can finish in a few evenings; it's easy cross stitching with a touch of backstitching and a few French/Colonial Knots. The flower stems are all backstitched with two threads of #877/13815. There are three French/Colonial Knots under the first yellow flower in front of the rabbit that are stitched with two threads of #1033/932. *Indicates placement. The rabbit's eye is a French/Colonial Knot that is stitched with one thread of #99/522 and one thread of #378/3773. Feel free to change fabrics, fibers, colors, add charms, etc. to make it your own piece.

Project Color Key

	DMC	ANCHOR	
○	225	893	Rose Wine
3	552	99	Violet
–	676	891	Brass
○	932	1033	Lt Antique Blue
6	3773	378	Md Fawn
●	3774	376	Lt Fawn
<	3817	875	Lt Pine
M	3815	877	Md Pine

P.O. Box 1347
Katy, TX 77492-1347
281-391-2281
fax 281-391-2290
e-mail: Moseynme2000@aol.com

❖ *Nordic Needle, Inc.*

Roz Watnemo

"HARDANGER EMBROIDERY DESIGN"

Stitch Count: 38 x 38

This piece was stitch on a piece of 5- x 5-inch 28-count antique white Cashel linen. The finished size is 2-3/4 x 2-3/4 inches. Fold the fabric to find the center point. From this point, count two threads to the right and 22 threads up to begin the first Satin Stitch block, using color #498 (see arrow). Work all of the Satin Stitch blocks. Cut and weave the bars in color #498. Use color #367 for the stem and leaf motifs. Use color #498 for the center lazy daisy and the flower motifs.

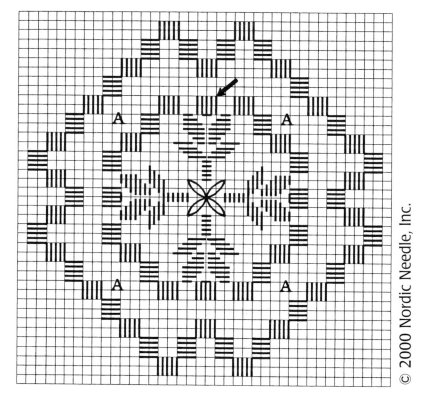

1314 Gateway Dr.
Fargo, ND 58103
701-235-5231 or 1-800-433-4321
fax 701-235-0952
e-mail: needle@corpcomm.net
website: www.nordicneedle.com

Project Color Key

DMC

❖ 367   Pistachio Green, dk (one ball #8 Pearl Cotton)

❖ 498   Christmas Red, dk (one ball #8 Pearl Cotton)

❖ *Northern Pine Designs*

Linda Lachance

"RAINBOW OVER THE PINES"

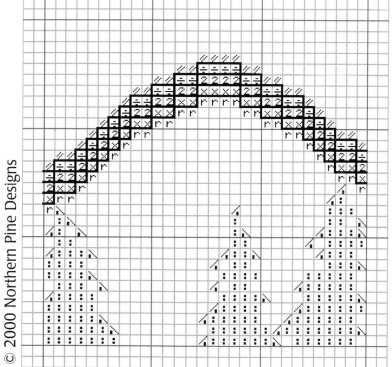

© 2000 Northern Pine Designs

Stitch Count: 30 x 30

This project was stitched over two on 28-count antique white Zweigart Jubilee. Two strands were used when stitching with DMC floss. Two strands were also used when backstitching with the Kreinik Blending Filament to create a magical sparkle in the rainbow. Be sure to keep your lengths of Blending Filament reasonably short to avoid tangling.

Project Color Key

	DMC	ANCHOR	
r	368	214	Pistachio Green Light
:	501	878	Blue Green Dark
▨	554	96	Violet Light
2	740	316	Tangerine
⊠	744	301	Yellow Pale
⊟	899	52	Rose Medium

❖ ▨ Backstitch with two strands of Kreinik 095 Stardust Blending Filament

Northern Pine Designs

1919 Overbrook Crescent,
Sudbury, Ontario, Canada
P3A 5H2
705-560-2919
website: http://home.accglobal.net/
~northern.pine

❖*Patricia Ann Designs*

Patricia Ann Bage

"LEVIATHAN FORGET-ME-KNOTS"

Stitch Count: 30 x 30

This project was stitched over two on antique white Cashel Linen. Work the Leviathan Stitch with two strands of DMC − 334. Backstitch with one strand of DMC − 501. Work Satin Stitch Blocks with one strand of DMC Perle Cotton #8 − Ecru. Cut and remove threads as indicated on the chart. Work Woven Bars over two threads and Dove's Eyes as indicated on the chart with one strand of DMC Perle Cotton #12 − Ecru.

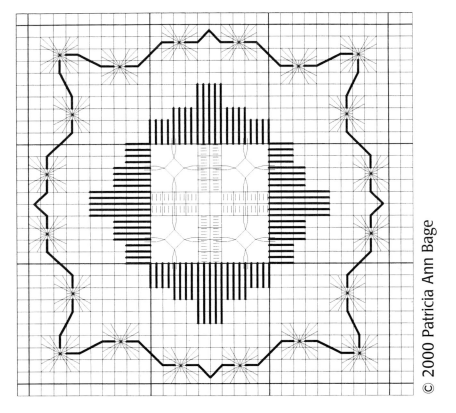

© 2000 Patricia Ann Bage

Project Color Key

	DMC	ANCHOR	
✔	334	977	Baby Blue - MD
▫	501	878	Blue Green - DK
❖	DMC Perle Cotton #8 − Ecru		
❖	DMC Perle Cotton #12 − Ecru		

Patricia Ann Designs
9 Poachers Close
Chatham, Kent, UK
MES82F

❖ *Paw Prints Cross Stitch*

Diana Huang

"STAINED GLASS BUTTERFLY"

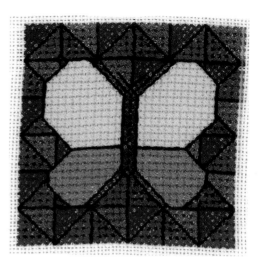

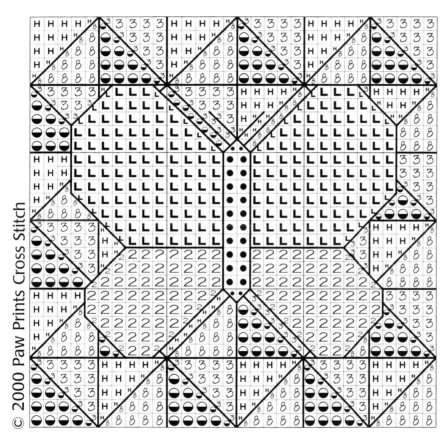

© 2000 Paw Prints Cross Stitch

Stitch Count: 30 x 30

This project was stitched on 28-count antique white Cashel linen using two strands of floss over two linen threads.

Project Color Key

	DMC	ANCHOR	
⊠	311	148	Naby Blue - MD
H	498	1005	Christmas Red - DK
⊡	552	99	Violet - MD
②	740	316	Tangerine
L	743	302	Yellow - MD
◒	890	218	Pistachio Green - UL DK
●	3031	360	Mocha Brown - VY DK
⊿	Backstitch done in two strands DMC 939		

Paw Prints Cross Stitch
1109 Worthington Woods Blvd.
Worthington, OH 43085
website:
www.pawprintscrossstitch.com

❖ *Purrfect Spots*

Nan Baker

"THE JADE TURTLE"

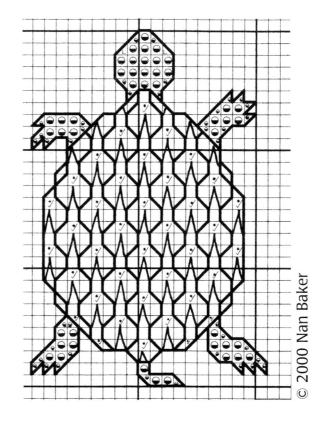

© 2000 Nan Baker

Stitch Count: 20 x 30

Separate six-strand floss into two strands for the design. First, backstitch the outline of the shell using two strands of DMC 367. Next do the Running Stitch as shown in Step 1 of The CASEY Stitch using two strands of DMC 368 (see the back of this book for all CASEY Stitch diagrams). Again, using two strands of floss, fill in the checks as shown in Step 2. Finish The CASEY Stitch with the arrow design as shown in Step 3 using one strand of DMC 890. Next, stitch the head, legs, and tail. Use two strands of DMC 890 to backstitch these. Backstitch the eyes using two strands of DMC 743.

While stitching this design, a giant sea turtle washed up on my beach. All species of sea turtles worldwide are threatened with extinction. Please check with conservation groups in your area to help save the turtles.

Project Color Key

	DMC	ANCHOR	
☑	367	217	Pistachio Green - dk
⊩	368	214	Pistachio Green - lt
⊡	743	302	Yellow - med
⊙	890	218	Pistachio Green - ul dk

Purrfect Spots
150 Betty St.
Santa Rosa Beach, FL 32459
e-mail: nan@purrfectspots.com

❖ *Risslee Designs*

Charity Thompson

"STAR CRYSTAL"

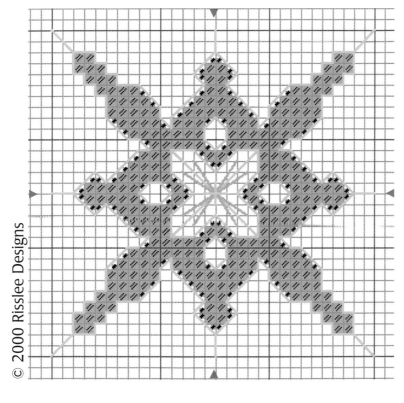

Stitch Count: 30 x 30

This project was stitched over two on 28-count antique white Zweigart Jubilee. Two strands were used when stitching with DMC floss. One strand was used when backstitching with the Kreinik Gold Cable. Be sure not to cut too long a length of cable or it will tangle.

For step-by-step instructions on how to complete the Tied Windmill Stitch in the center of this star, please see the stitch diagrams at the back of this book.

Project Color Key

	DMC	ANCHOR	
☑	554	96	Violet Light
☑	554	96	Step 2 of Tied Windmill Stitch done with two strands of Violet Light

❖ ☑ Backstitching around star as well as Steps 1 and 3 of the Tied Windmill Stitch are done with one strand of Kreinik 002P Gold Cord.

Risslee Designs
P.O. Box 702, Station Main,
Abbotsford, British Columbia, Canada
V2S 6R7
e-mail: service@risslee.com
website: www.risslee.com

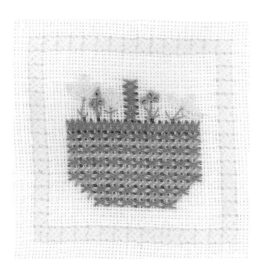

❖ Sekas & Co.

Sue Stehie

"A SPRING BASKET"

Stitch Count: 30 x 30

This project was stitched over two on antique white Cashel Linen.

1. Stitch the border with Woven Cross over four threads using two strands of 3823.

2. Stitch the basket handle with Horizontal Oblong Cross using two strands of 3829.

3. Stitch the basket rim with Vertical Oblong Cross using two strands of 3829.

4. The main part of the basket is stitched with alternating rows of Horizontal Oblong Cross (as indicated below) using two strands of 3829 and Half Cross using two strands of 729.

5. Plant stems are Long Stitches using one strand of 502.

6. Flowers on stems one, three, and five are Lazy Daisy using two strands of 819.

7. Flowers on stems two and four are (*) French Knots using two strands of 932.

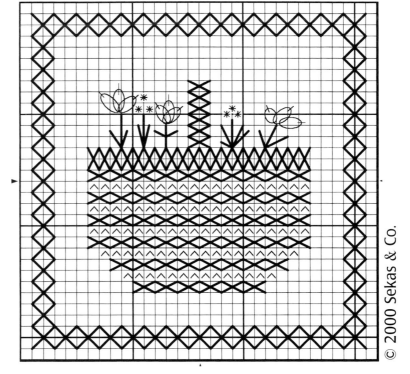

© 2000 Sekas & Co.

Project Color Key

	DMC	ANCHOR	
	502	877	Blue Green
⌧	729	890	Old Gold - med (1/2 stitch)
	819	271	Baby Pink - lt
	932	1033	Antique Blue - lt
	3823	386	Ultra Pale Yellow
	3829	901	Old Gold - vy dk

Sekas & Co.
1114 N. Court #112
Medina, OH 44256
1-800-714-5513

❖ *Something In Common Designs*

Barbara Peterson

'MORNIN' ALL"

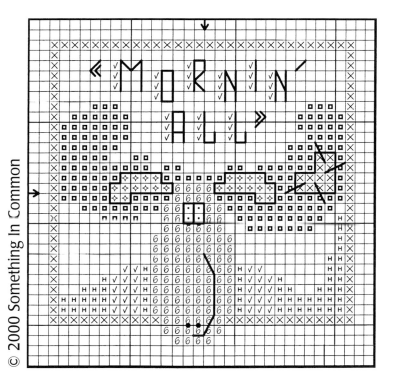

© 2000 Something In Common

Stitch Count: 30 x 30

This project was stitched on 28-count antique white Cashel Linen. The stitched design size is 2 x 2 inches. Use two strands of floss for all cross stitches and one strand for backstitches. French Knots are done with one strand of floss with two twists around the needle (represented by large dots for the eyes and nostrils).

Project Color Key

	DMC	ANCHOR	
☑	367	217	Pistachio Green - dk
⊞	498	1005	Christmas Red - dk
⊠	744	301	Yellow - pale
▣	839	360	Beige Brown - dk
⑤	841	378	Beige Brown - lt
⊡	842	388	Beige Brown - vy lt
☑	844	1041	Beaver Brown - ul dk
·	5200	1	Snow White

Floss Used for Backstitches & French Knot:

	DMC	ANCHOR	
◪	498	1005	Words, heart (on antler)
◪	844	1041	Ears, eyes, and smile
•	844	1041	French Knots for eyes and nose

Something In Common
P.O. Box 872
Wausau, WI 54402-0872
715-842-0266
fax 715-845-9289
e-mail: SICBP@aol.com
website: www.somethingincom.com

Stitch Count: 29w x 42h

This project was stitched over one on 28-count antique white linen using a variety of fibers.

Row 1: Cross stitch using one strand each of DMC 311, 552, and 676.

Row 2: Backstitch the words using two strands of DMC 500.

Row 3: Cross stitch using two strands of DMC 676.

Row 4: Satin Stitch the heart using two strands of DMC 552, then go over every other using Kreinik very fine braid Purple 012C.

Row 5: Chain Stitch using two strands of DMC 839.

Row 6: Backstitch the Infinity sign using two strands of DMC 500 and then go over using Kreinik very fine braid Green 008 HL.

Row 7: Satin Stitch using two strands of DMC 311. Backstitch around in Kreinik tapestry braid Confetti Fuschia 042.

Spirit of Design
630 Kirkwood Hwy. A-1
Newark, DE 19711
e-mail: JALWMS@aol.com

❖ *Spirit of Design*

Anna Navarro-Williams

"INFINITE LOVE"

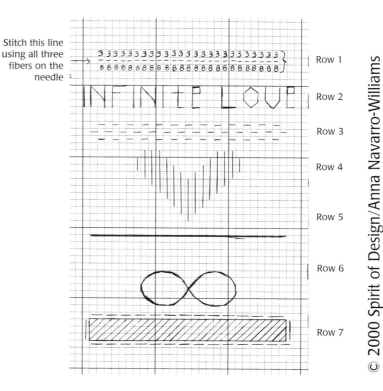

Stitch this line using all three fibers on the needle

Row 1
Row 2
Row 3
Row 4
Row 5
Row 6
Row 7

© 2000 Spirit of Design/Anna Navarro-Williams

Project Color Key

	DMC	ANCHOR	
▨	552	99	Violet - med
▨	311	148	Navy Blue - med
◪	500	683	Blue Green - vy dk
▣	839	360	Beige Brown - dk
⊟	676	891	Old Gold - lt

❖ Kreinik 042 Confetti Fuschia Tapestry Braid

❖ Kreinik 008HL Green Very Fine Braid

❖ Kreinik 012C Purple Very Fine Braid

❖ *Stitchin' Station*

Betsy Hanson

"MINI BAND SAMPLER"

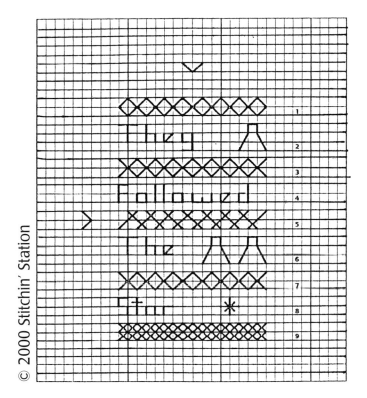

Project Color Key

- ❖ Splendor #5822
- ❖ Splendor #5832
- ❖ Dark Ruby Aztecs by Gumnut
- ❖ Stars #369 by Gumnut
- ❖ Kreinik 002 Gold #4 Very Fine Braid

© 2000 Stitchin' Station

Stitch Count: 16w x 28h

This project was stitched over two on 28-count antique white Cashel Linen using a variety of wonderful fibers.

Band 1: Queen Stitch worked in one strand of Splendor #S822.

Bands 2, 4, 6 and 8: All of the words are backstitched with two strands of Splendor #S832.

Band 2: The wise man is backstitched in two strands of Aztecs, dark ruby, by Gumnut.

Band 3: Plaited Stitch worked in one strand of Stars #369 by Gumnut.

Band 5: Herringbone Stitch worked in two strands of Aztecs, dark ruby, by Gumnut.

Band 6: The first wise man is backstitched in two strands of Splendor #822, and the second wise man is worked in two strands of Stars #369 by Gumnut.

Band 7: Algerian Eyelet worked with one strand of #4 Kreinik braid #002.

Band 8: The star is worked in a Star Stitch with one strand of #4 Kreinik braid #002.

Band 9: Rice Stitch worked with one strand of Splendor #822.

Stitchin' Station

15 McCauley Dr.
Salem, VA 24153
540-389-5733

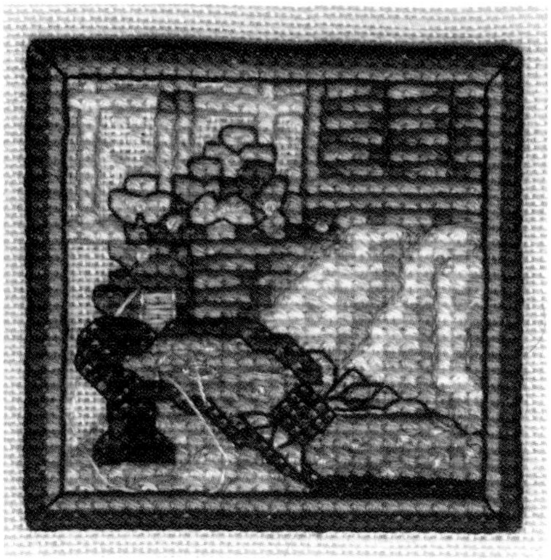

❖ *Teixeira*

Nellie Teixeira

"YESTERDAY, TODAY & TOMORROW"

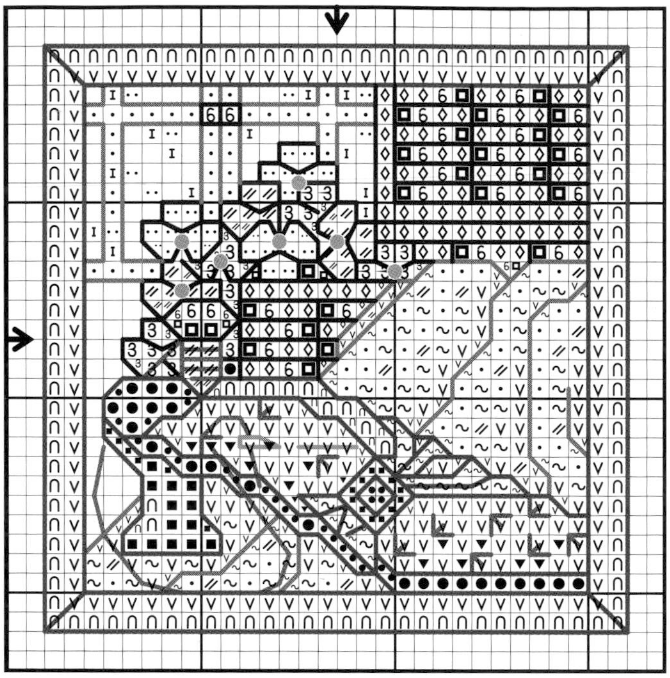

Stitch Count: 30 x 30

This project was stitched over two threads on 28-count antique white Zweigart Cashel Linen.

Project Color Key

	DMC	ANCHOR	
■	550	102	Violet - vy dk
3	552	99	Violet - med
▨	554	96	Violet - lt
··	819	271	Baby Pink - lt
▣	839	360	Beige Brown - dk
6	841	378	Beige Brown - lt
◇	842	388	Beige Brown - vy lt
▼	931	1034	Antique Blue - med
V	932	1033	Antique Blue - lt
■	939	152	Navy Blue - vy dk
I	3072	847	Beaver Grey - vy lt
∩	3750	1036	Antique Blue - vy dk
~	3753	1031	Antique Blue - ul vy lt
	B5200		Snow White

Floss Used for Backstitches & French Knots:

◪	550	102	Outline of flowers
◪	554	96	Outside embroidered shoe stitches
◪	819	271	Long thread, bobbin, inside show stitches
◪	931	1034	Outline of blanket, window
◪	939	152	Outline of shoe, buckle, border
◪	3031	360	Basket, bobbin top, window knobs
◪	5283		Needle
•	676	891	Flower Center

Johannesburg, South Africa
published by CraftSoft, Inc.
981 Wellington Rd. S., Suite 501
London, Ontario, Canada N6E 3A9
e-maiL: info@craftsoft.com
website: www.craftsoft.com

Teixeira Designs

❖ *Textured Treasures*

Karen E. Dudzinski

"ROYAL GLORY"

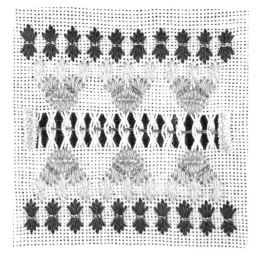

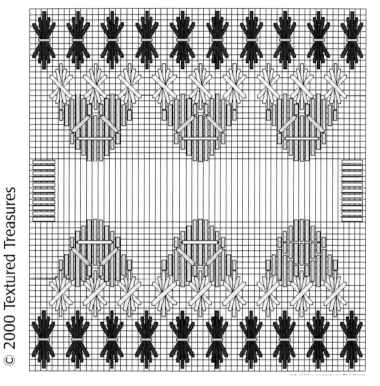

© 2000 Textured Treasures

Stitch Count: 60 x 60

This project was stitched over one on 28-count antique white Zweigart Cashel Linen.

1. Begin by stitching the sheaves with two strands of DMC 3750. The binding of each sheaf is done with a double strand of DMC 5282 gold metallic floss.

2. Continue onto the next row, consisting of partial Rhodes Stitches completed with two strands of DMC 3753.

3. The "crowns" are to be Satin Stitched with two strands of DMC 729. Note that on the chart, one crown is illustrated without the accent stitches to act as a guide for Satin Stitch placement. The long accent stitch is done with a single strand of DMC 676 #8 Pearl Cotton, while the two smaller accent stitches are done with a doubled strand of DMC 5282 gold metallic floss.

4. To complete the drawn thread area, first lay the binding blocks on the left and right with a single strand of DMC 676 #8 Pearl Cotton. After cutting and removing the fabric threads from this area, use a double strand of DMC gold metallic to interlace as shown in the stitch diagrams at the back of the book.

Project Color Key

	DMC	ANCHOR	
☑	729	890	Two strands of Old Gold Medium
❖ 🔲	3750	1036	Two strands of Antique Blue V. Dark
☑	3753	1031	Two strands of Ant. Blue Ultra V. light
❖	DMC 5282 Gold Metallic floss		
❖	DMC 676 Pearl Cotton #8		

Textured Treasures
14 Mugford Road,
Aurora, Ontario, Canada
L4G 7H3
e-mail: ttreasures2000@yahoo.ca
website: www.texturedtreasures.com

A Celebration of Stitching

75

❖ *The Stitcher's Habit*

Carol Scott Higeli

"MOOSE XING"

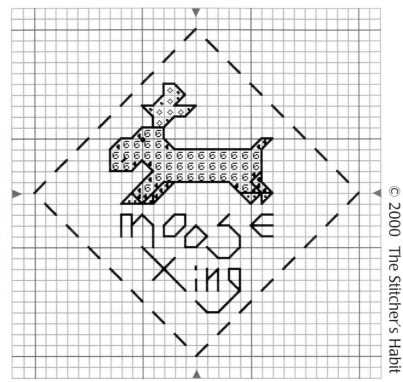

Stitch Count: 30 x 30

This project was stitched over two threads on 28-count antique white Zweigart Cashel Linen. Two strands of DMC floss were used, except to attach the tiny black Mill Hill bead for the eye. This can also be done with a French Knot in one or two strands of floss, depending on your preference.

© 2000 The Stitcher's Habit

Project Color Key

	DMC	ANCHOR	
⑤	841	378	Beige Brown Light
◈	842	388	Beige Brown Very Light
⊡	3031	360	Mocha Brown Very Dark
▨			Border done in a Running Stitch with one strand of DMC 498/Anchor 1005
▨			Backstitching around Moose & lettering done with one strand of DMC 498/Anchor 1005
❖ ●			Mill Hill 42014-1 bead attached with one strand of DMC 498/Anchor 1005 (Note: A French Knot may also be used)

The Stitcher's Habit

P.O. Box 86,
Greenbank, Ontario, Canada
L0C 1B0
website: www.stitchershabit.com
e-mail: carol@stitchershabit.com

❖ *A Dozen Ideas*

Great Ways to Use the Squares in This Book

Afghans or Quilt Blocks
Because the colors are all coordinated, you can pick out enough squares to fit almost any project on Anne cloth or other afghan materials.

Cards

Chatelaines

Coasters

Keepsake Boxes

Needlecase Covers

Needlerolls
Select two of your favorite squares that use intricate geometric techniques like drawn thread, hardanger, beading, etc., or repeat the same square twice, side by side, to create a needleroll.

Ornaments
Stitch them up one at a time or create a whole tree's worth! These are just the right size for ornament exchanges. Best of all, they can be kept out all year long.

Pillows
Switch any of these designs to a larger count fabric and you've got pillows or sachets.

Round Robins
No more searching for things to use! These tiny squares offer so many different images and techniques that you are sure to find something to inspire you.

Scissor Fobs

Wearables
Work up a square on pre-made clothing that has a stitchable panel or use waste canvas to transfer the design to a sweatshirt, jacket, etc.

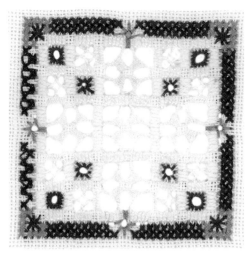

❖ *Threads of Grace*

Karen A. Wellman

"HARDANGER SQUARE"

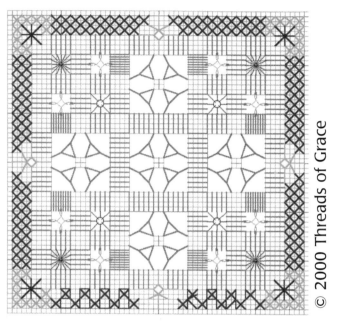

Stitch Count: 60 x 60

Jim and I are very happy to contribute to this collection. Our design is for the intermediate stitcher who loves Hardanger.

Your work will cover 60 x 60 threads and has a variety of stitches. Each graph square equals one linen thread.

The five Satin Stitches making the kloster blocks, Dove's Eyes, and Greek Cross are shown in gray only for printing purposes. The gray indicates White (5200) Pearl Cotton. The Dove's Eye, needle weaving, and Greek Cross Filling are done with #12, 5200 pearl cotton. The kloster blocks are done with #8, 5200 pearl cotton.

The corners to our border are done in gold (3829). The sides are done in checkerboard red (814) and green (890).

The Smyrna Cross, Eyelet, and Algerian Eye are done in blue (311).

1. Complete all of the kloster blocks.
2. Complete the cross stitch border and gold eyelet variation.
3. You need to complete the Smyrna Cross, Eyelet, and Algerian Eye.

4. Do the cut work for the Hardanger, taking care when cutting. The area for the Dove's Eyes and Greek Cross are the cut out areas.
5. Do the needle weaving, Greek Crosses, and Dove's Eyes.
6. You may now trim and finish to your preference. You could make a sachet, Christmas ornament, or pin cushion.

May all your threads be stitched with grace.

Threads of *Grace*

100 Chapel View Dr.
Reinholds, PA 17569
717-336-6334
e-mail: jwellman@ptd.net
website: www.threadsofgrace.com

Project Color Key

DMC	ANCHOR	
311	148	Navy Blue - med
814	45	Garnet - dk
890	218	Pistachio Green - ul dk
3829	901	Old Gold - vy dk
❖ #8 White DMC Pearl Cotton		
❖ #12 White DMC Pearl Cotton		

❖ *Tink Boord-Dill Needlework*

Tink Boord-Dill

"AUTUMN ACORN"

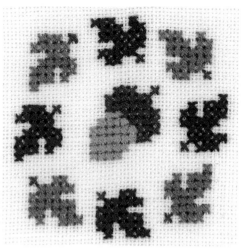

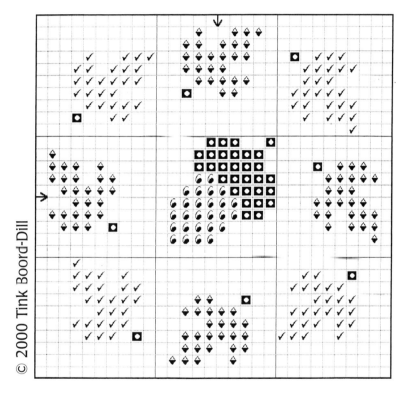

© 2000 Tink Boord-Dill

Stitch Count: 30 x 30

This project was stitched over two on 28-count antique white Cashel Linen using two strands of floss.

ORIGINAL DESIGNS

Project Color Key

☑	367	217	Pistachio Grn-DK
▣	839	360	Beige Brown-DK
⑤	841	378	Beige Brown-LT
▣	890	218	Pistachio Grn-UL DK

P.O. Box 1046
Richmond, KY 40476-1046
859-624-3525
fax 859-623-5566
e-mail: web@tinkbd.com
website: www.tinkbd.com

"SHALOM: PEACE TO ALL"

Stitch Count: 30 x 30

This project was stitched on 28-count antique white Zweigart Cashel Linen. Alternate: Charles Craft 14-count antique white Aida cloth.

Instructions: Use four strands of floss in cross stitches. This creates very full, raised stitches, resembling a pebble mosaic which covers the fabric completely. If you want a more traditional cross stitch look, or if you have difficulty passing the needle, decrease to two or three strands of floss.

Tip: If working with four strands of floss, try using a size 9 crewel needle. This has a medium size eye and a sharp point, both of which help the needle slide through this tight stitchery. If working two or three strands, try using a size 26 or 28 tapestry needle with a larger eye and blunt point.

To create a rich, uniform look, work the blue floss first and then fill in with the red. Work each section separately, including each letter, weaving in the thread ends on the reverse as you go.

The finished piece may be framed or made into an ornament. Hang this in your entryway as a blessing for your visitors, *Peace to All*.

P.O. Box 2208
Rockville, MD 20847-2208

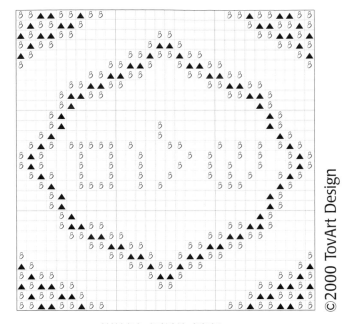

©2000 TovArt Design

חסד-ואמת נפגשו
צדק ושלום נשקו

Loving kindness and truth have met;
justice and peach have kissed.
Psalm 85:11

Psalm 85 is a prayer for the prophetic vision of redemption, when loving kindness, truth, justice, and peace will bless the world. This stitchery with the Hebrew word for peace, *shalom*, reminds us to strive for this divine quality in our everyday life.

Unlike English, Hebrew is written from right to left. The letters in this word are שׁ shin, ל lamed, ו vav, ם mem.

Project Color Key

	DMC	ANCHOR	
Six-strand cotton floss			
⊠	311	148	Navy Blue - med
▲	814	45	Garnet - dk

❖ Treasured Tapestries

Dianne Durgan Sobolewski

"SCARECROW FRIEND"

© 2000 Dianne Durgan Sobolewski

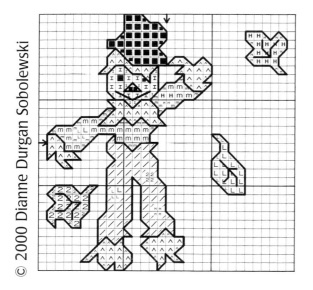

Project Color Key

	DMC	ANCHOR	
✏	334	977	Baby Blue-med.
H	498	1005	Christmas Red-dk.
M	502	877	Blue Green
∧	729	890	Old Gold-med.
2	740	316	Tangerine
L	743	302	Yellow-med.
■	939	152	Navy Blue-vy. dk.
I	3072	847	Beaver Grey-vy. lt.

Cross Stitches: x2
Backstitching: x1
740-mouth
839-straw at neck, hair, hands, feet, leaves
939-hat, head, nose, shirt, pants
3/4 and 1/4 (split) stitches: x2 Always work
the 3/4 stitch for whatever is on (in front)
in design, and the 1/4 stitch for whatever is
underneath (in back) in the design.
Patches: work in 3/4 stitches.

Stitch Count: 30 x 30

This project was stitched on a 2-1/8- x 2-1/8-inch piece of 28-count antique white Cashel Linen. Use 15-inch lengths of floss. Before beginning, let the floss strands hang separately to untwist the strands, then thread the needle. Hold a 1-inch tail of floss on the back of the design and work the first few to secure. When finishing a length of floss, run under the back to secure. Never carry floss across blank spaces of fabric because they will show through on the front. Always cross all of your stitches in the same direction throughout the design for a nice, uniform appearance.

Finish the edges of the fabric with machine zigzag, hand overcast, or masking tape. Fold fabric in half lengthwise; crease with your thumb. This will be your vertical center line. Find the arrow at the top center of the chart and count how many grid squares you need to go down or across to begin first stitch. Measure down 3 inches from fabric top center, plus grid squares counted. Mark this spot on fabric with a pin or extra needle and begin stitching here. If you prefer starting the design in the center of chart, this is fine, also.

There are many options for finishing the design besides the usual method of mat and framing: Halloween treat bag; child or adult top/jacket; stuffed pillow; tote bag; felt-backed ornament; quilt square; pin; baby bib/top/jacket.

6 Timber Trail, P.O. Box 225
Cobalt, CT 06414-0225
fax: 860-267-8042
e-mail:
dianne.sobolewski@prodigy.net

❖ *Twisted Threads*

Ruth Sparrow

"FLOWERS FOR A FRIEND"

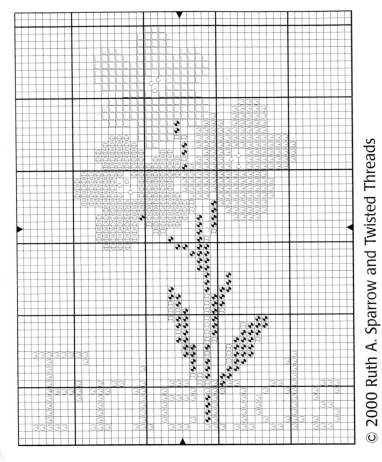

Stitch Count: 43 x 56

This project was stitched over one on 28-count antique white Cashel linen. All cross stitch is done over one linen thread with one strand of floss. Colonial (or French) Knots: Use four strands of floss. Each flower gets three knots in the center. The center of the rose flower is done with yellow knots. The center of the violet flower is done with rose knots. The center of the yellow flower is done with violet knots.

7013 Miami Avenue
Cincinnati, OH 45243
513-271-7703
e-mail: twistedshop@aol.com
website: www.twistedthreads.com

Project Color Key

	DMC	ANCHOR	
⊠	309	42	Rose - deep
ꞁ	368	214	Pistachio Green - lt
③	552	99	Violet - med
ㄥ	743	302	Yellow - med
⊡	890	218	Pistachio Green - ul dk

❖ *Ursula Michael Designs*

Ursula Michael

"WILD ROSES QUILT SQUARE"

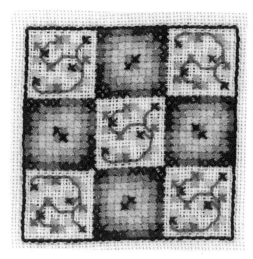

Stitch Count: 30 x 30

This project was stitched over two on 28-count antique white Cashel Linen with two strands of floss.

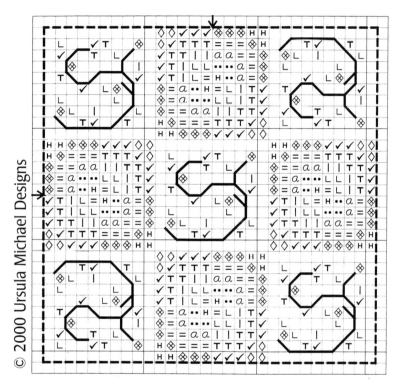

© 2000 Ursula Michael Designs

Project Color Key

	DMC	ANCHOR	
⊗	309	42	Rose-DK
☑	367	217	Pistachio GM-DK
⊓	368	214	Pistachio Green-LT
Ⅰ	369	1043	Pistachio Grn-VY LT
H	498	1005	Christmas Red-DK
L	743	302	Yellow-MD
a	776	24	Pink-MD
··	819	271	Baby Pink-LT
◈	890	218	Pistachio GM-UL DK
=	899	52	Rose-MD

Floss Used for Backstitches:

◿	367	217	Pistachio Grn-DK
◿	498	1005	Christmas Red-DK

Ursula Michael Designs
54 Bigelow Rd.
Colchester, CT 06415
860-267-4835
fax 860-267-7464
e-mail: ursula@snet.net

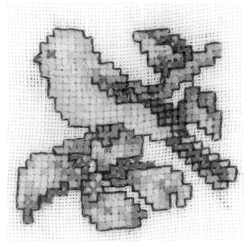

Vickery Collection

Mike Vickery

"SPRING BIRD"

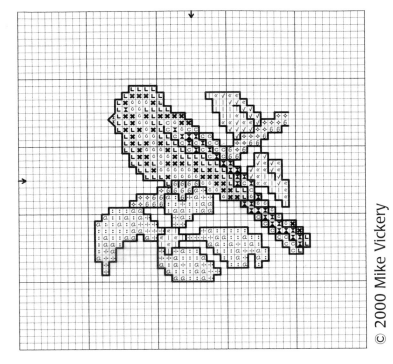

Stitch Count: 31w x 29h

This project was stitched over two on 28-count antique white Cashel Linen using two strands of floss. One strand was used for the backstitching.

Project Color Key

	DMC	ANCHOR	
☑	367	217	Pistachio Green - dk
⌐	368	214	Pistachio Green - lt
Ⅱ	369	1043	Pistachio Green - vy lt
Ⅹ	646	8581	Beaver Grey - dk
C	648	900	Beaver Grey - lt
L	743	302	Yellow - med

	DMC	ANCHOR	
⊠	744	301	Yellow - pale
ɑ	776	24	Pink - med
⊡	819	271	Baby Pink - lt
6	841	378	Beige Brown - lt
⊗	842	388	Beige Brown - vy lt
⊟	899	52	Rose - med
▣	3823	386	Ultra Pale Yellow

Backstitches:

	DMC	ANCHOR	
◿	844	1041	Beaver Grey - ul dk

Vickery Collection
302 Bozeman Rd.
White, GA 30184
e-mail: m-avickery@worldnet.att.net
website: www.stitching.com/
vickerycollection

❖ *Web Stitch*

Moana Bianchin

"LOVE TO STITCH"

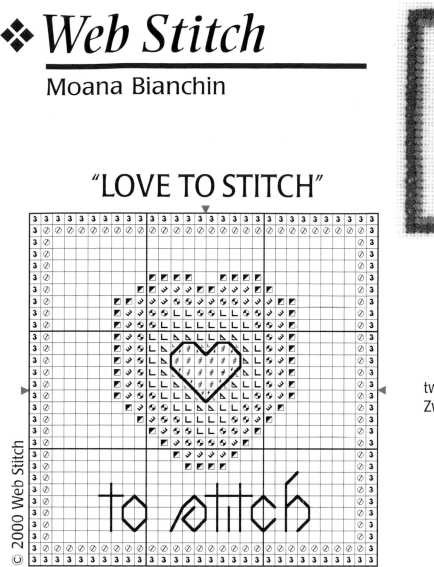

Stitch Count: 30 x 30

This project was stitched over two on 28-count antique white Zweigart Cashel Linen.

© 2000 Web Stitch

Project Color Key

Two strands dk Christmas Red

◣ Blend one strand med yellow (743) and one strand tangerine (740)

∟ Two strands med yellow (743)

◔ Blend one strand med yellow (743) and one strand lt pistachio green (368)

➔ Blend one strand lt pistachio green (368) and one strand med baby blue (334)

◢ Blend one strand med baby blue (334) and one strand lt violet (554)

⊘ Two strands med rose (899)

3 Two strands med violet (552)

Backstitches:

╱ Heart use one strand Christmas red (498)

"To stitch" use 1 str med violet (552)

Oropi R.D.3 Tauranga
3021 New Zealand
Ph/Fax: 0064 7 5431478
e-mail: moana.oropi@clear.net.nz
website: www.webstitch.co.nz

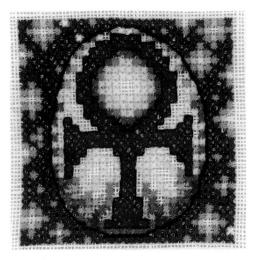

❖ *Witches Stitches*

Anne Marie Garrison and Becca Allen

"SACRED ANKH"

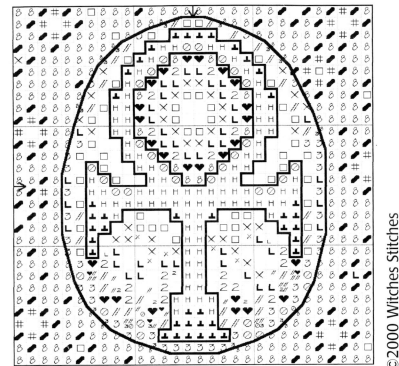

Stitch Count: 30 x 30

This project was stitched by Becca Allen over two on 28-count antique white Cashel Linen using two strands of DMC floss. One strand of DMC 939 was used for all of the backstitching.

©2000 Witches Stitches

Project Color Key

	DMC	ANCHOR	
◙	309	42	Rose - deep
8	311	148	Navy Blue - med
∕	334	977	Baby Blue - med
H	498	1005	Christmas Red - dk
3	552	99	Violet - med

	DMC	ANCHOR	
⊘	554	96	Violet - lt
2	740	316	Tangerine
L	743	302	Yellow - med
✕	744	301	Yellow - pale
▲	814	45	Garnet - dk
♥	947	330	Burnt Orange
▦	3325	129	Baby Blue - lt
▢	3823	386	Ultra Pale Yellow

Witches Stitches
P.O. Box 6858
Minneapolis, MN 55406
612-823-1079
e-mail: wstitches@herakles.com
website: www.witchesstitches.com

Wren Song Designs

Dorothy Gilchrist

"ROSE WREATH"

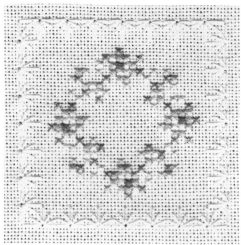

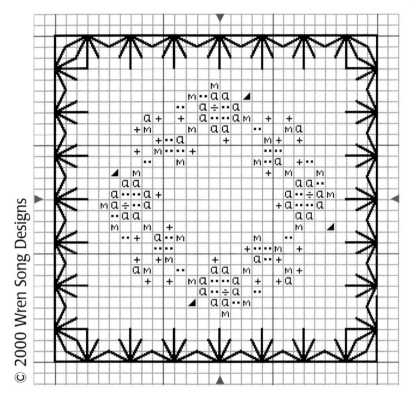

© 2000 Wren Song Designs

Stitch Count: 30 x 30

This project was stitched over two on 28-count antique white Zweigart Jubilee. Two strands were used when stitching with the pink colors of DMC floss but only one strand of the DMC greens. One strand was used when stitching with the Kreinik #4 Very Fine Braid. A single strand of the DMC #12 White Pearl Cotton was also used for the Partial Diamond Eyelet Stitches, indicated in backstitching on the chart. For more details on completing this stitch, please refer to the stitch diagrams at the back of this book.

Project Color Key

	DMC	ANCHOR	
M	502	877	One strand of Blue Green
+	504	1042	One strand of Blue Green Very Light
Q	776	24	Two strands of Pink Medium
⋅⋅	819	271	Two strands of Baby Pink Light
÷	899	52	Two strands of Rose Medium
❖ ◢	001HL Silver Kreinik #4 Very Fine Braid
❖ ◩	Backstitch with one strand of DMC Pearl Cotton #12 White

Wren Song Designs
317 Begg Crescent
Saskatoon, Saskatchewan, Canada
S7H 4P3
306-373-8056
e-mail: wrenson_ca@yahoo.co.uk

❖ *X's & Oh's*

Joanne Gatenby

"CHICKADEE"

© 2000 X's & Oh's

Stitch Count: 30 x 30

This project was stitched over-backstitch two on 28-count antique white Zweigart Jubilee. Three strands were used when stitching with the DMC floss, while two strands were used for the CARON Wildflowers. Regular floss may also be used for the pine sprig.

ORIGINAL CROSS-STITCH DESIGNS

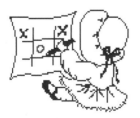

134 Lake Street,
Mallorytown, Ontario, Canada
K0E 1R0
e-mail: xs_and_ohs@cybertap.com
website:
www.cybertap.com/bgatenby/xsandohs/

Project Color Key

	DMC	ANCHOR	
⌐	368	214	Pistachio Green light
H	498	1005	Christmas Red Dark
I	646	8581	Beaver Grey Dark
C	648	900	Beaver Grey Light
◇	842	388	Beige Brown Very Light
Z	844	1041	Beaver Grey Ultra Dark
·	5200	1	Snow White

❖ ▨ Stitch with two strands of Caron Black Wildflowers

▨ Backstitch bird and berry stem with one strand of DMC 844/Anchor 1041

❖ ▨ Long Stitches in pine sprig done with two strands of Caron Moss Wildflowers

● French Knot in one strand of Black Wildflowers

❖ Stitch Diagrams

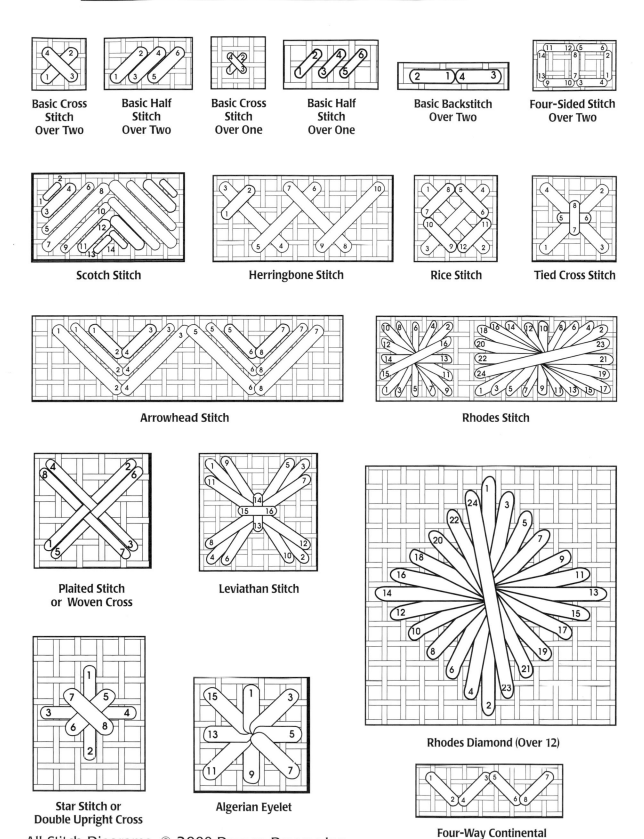

Basic Cross Stitch Over Two

Basic Half Stitch Over Two

Basic Cross Stitch Over One

Basic Half Stitch Over One

Basic Backstitch Over Two

Four-Sided Stitch Over Two

Scotch Stitch

Herringbone Stitch

Rice Stitch

Tied Cross Stitch

Arrowhead Stitch

Rhodes Stitch

Plaited Stitch or Woven Cross

Leviathan Stitch

Rhodes Diamond (Over 12)

Star Stitch or Double Upright Cross

Algerian Eyelet

Four-Way Continental

All Stitch Diagrams © 2000 Dragon Dreams Inc.

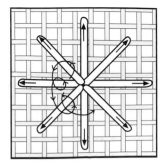

Ribbed Spider's Web

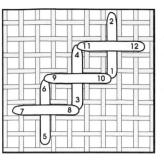

Diagonal Upright Cross Stitch

Waffle Stitch

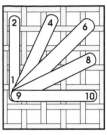

Double Leviathan Stitch

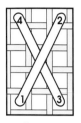

Vertical Oblong Cross Stitch

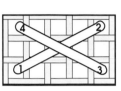

Horizontal Oblong Cross Stitch

Half Diamond Eyelet

Fan Stitch

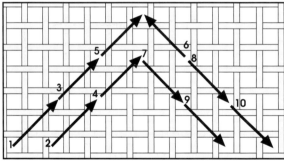

Cable Stitch

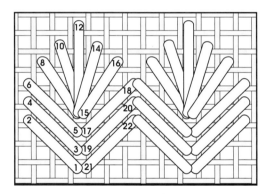

Leaf Stitch

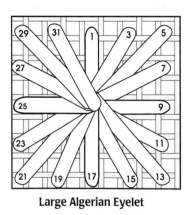

Large Algerian Eyelet

Diagonal Mosaic

Roman Cross Variation

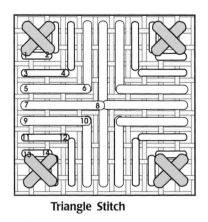

Triangle Stitch

All Stitch Diagrams © 2000 Dragon Dreams Inc.

A Celebration of Stitching

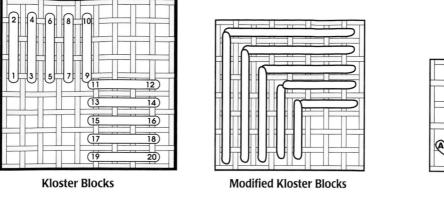

Kloster Blocks

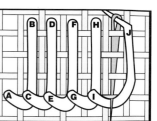

Modified Kloster Blocks

Buttonhole Stitch

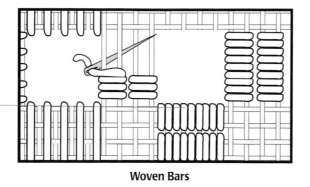

Woven Bars

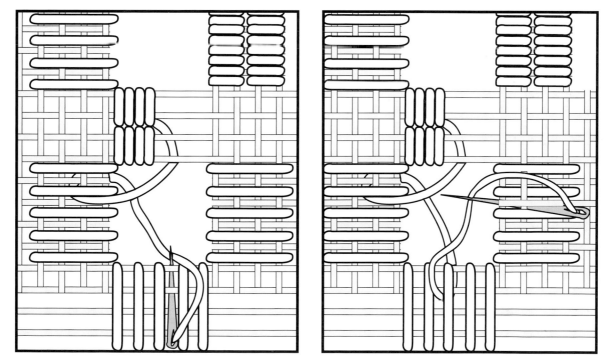

Dove's Eye Part One

Dove's Eye Part Two (Continue Woven Bars)

All Stitch Diagrams © 2000 Dragon Dreams Inc.

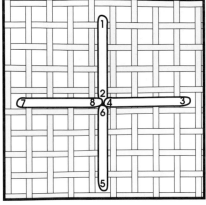

Tied Windmill Stitch Step One
(use Gold Cable for Risslee Designs)

Tied Windmill Stitch Step Two
(use two strands DMC 554 for Risslee Designs)

Tied Windmill Stitch Step Three
(use Gold Cable for Risslee Designs)

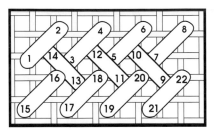

Woven Plait

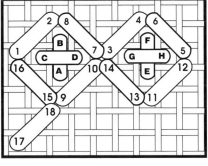

Lattice Stitch

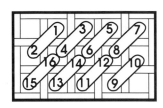

**Basic Continental
Tent Stitch**

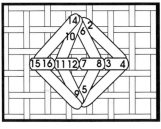

Queen Stitch

Smyrna Cross

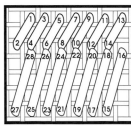

Gobelin Stitch

Hungarian Stitch

All Stitch Diagrams © 2000 Dragon Dreams Inc.

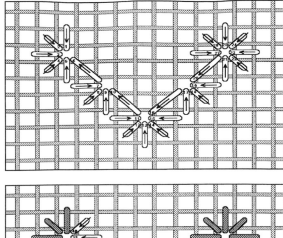

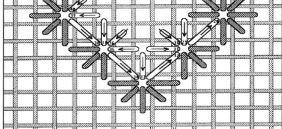

The joined eyelets are stitched by the diagrams above. The top diagram shows the beginning of the trip around all of the eyelets. The stitch that joins the eyelets is actually stitched twice. In the bottom diagram, the darker colored stitches are those of the top diagram that are already done, and the numbering continues to complete the eyelets.

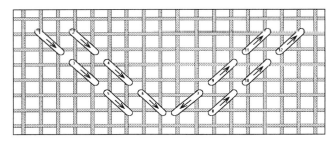

This shows the turning of the reverse double faggot stitch. Begin this stitch at one of the corners beside the eyelets, stitching the outside row of reverse faggot stitches as shown. Once all four sides of the diamond shape are done, refer to the diagram below on how to turn and complete the row.

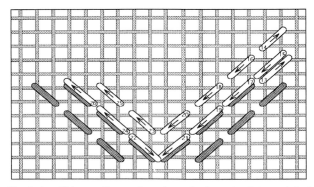

The darker stitches are the ones from above that have already been stitched. When all four sides are complete, do a backstitch (#14) to begin the next row. Then head back in the direction you came from, laying a second stitch in the same holes that the ones from the previous round are in as shown. (This side is shown shorter than the actual chart for explanation purposes.)

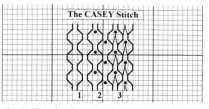

The CASEY Stitch is worked in three steps. First, outline or backstitch the design and then fill in by stitching the running stitch as shown in Step 1. Next, stitch the dots (Step 2) and then stitch the arrow design (Step 3). Stitching the steps in order will make the design easier to follow and finish.

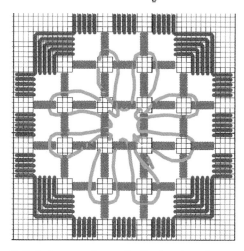

A. First, weave counterclockwise. Begin at the arrow.

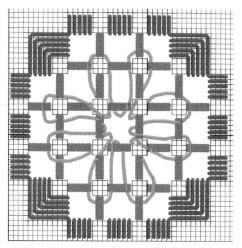

B. Clockwise weave. Reverse the direction of weaving at the arrow.

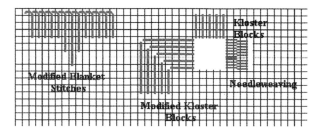

Index

❖ *Thank You*

From Jennifer L. Aikman-Smith

Sometimes, getting things from inspiration to tangible stage is a bit more work than you anticipated... make that a lot more work! This project would never have been possible without the hard work of several people and companies who deserve to be thanked—and this is my chance to do just that.

❖ To my fellow INRG Legal Defense Fund Committee Members: Cheri, Tink, Peg, Sharon, Jim, and Letha. Thank you for helping refine my ramblings and catch those spelling differences between Canadian and American English. Jim, thank you for doing all of the interviews and getting this issue the attention it needs. Thank you for your support and help in the midst of becoming a grandfather! Letha, thank you for letting your house and your itty bitty postal box act as the focal point for the USA mailings. I hope your post office manager has calmed down now. Thank you as well for all of the scanning and compiling of names and addresses needed to get this project to the lay-out stage.

❖ To Pat Klug, Amy Tincher-Durik, and all of the layout elves at Krause, without whom this book would have remained just an inspiration. Thank you for all of the help, the games of phone tag, the laughter over insane deadlines, and the shared belief that pro-tecting our industry with a project like this was important enough to be worth all of the craziness.

❖ To Jill at DMC: Thank you for your help in narrowing the original Master List down to a manageable size. Your input on color availability from coast to coast and internation-ally was greatly appreciated.

❖ To Jim at Zweigart: Thank you for mailing out little squares of Jubilee and Cashel Linen all over the place to make sure designers had a common product to work on if they didn't have any in their stash.

❖ To Lane and Rod at Hoffman Distributing: Thank you for your patience as Storm Bringer got bumped around with my grandmother's death and the *Celebration* dead-lines. I appreciate your flexibility, understanding, and support of this worthy cause.

❖ To my beloved husband, Nick: Thank you for putting up with all of the late nights, for stitching up models so quickly, for cooking suppers or reading bedtime stories to Erin and Bethany when I was down in my "dungeon" on the computer, and for keeping me grounded through some very stormy months.

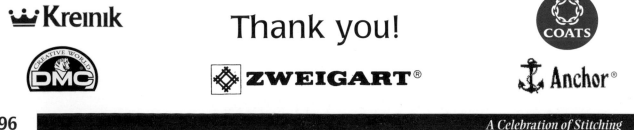

Thank you!

96 A Celebration of Stitching